Becoming a Boss Lady Real Estate Investor

KRISTA GOODRICH

ISBN: 979-8-9939897-0-9 (paperback)
979-8-9939897-1-6 (eBook)

5 Star Reviews *for*
Becoming a Boss Lady Real Estate Investor

If you are ready to level-up your portfolio, and your life, grab this book today. This book shares the tools every Boss Lady needs to become a real estate investor and to create the life of her dreams.

— Kym Nguyen

To the women who carry our family's financial future ... This book is your blueprint for generational financial freedom. The core lesson is a profound mindset shift: trading self-doubt for the internal roar of "Watch Me". This is how you stop waiting for permission and build a life of financial freedom on your own terms.

— Bill Ryser

I am obsessed with the thought that I can actually read this and take something from it because, as a woman, I feel like finances is such a male dominated area. This book provides me the hope and encouragement that this is stuff that I can understand, and I can make money without having to "be with a man".

— Shea Tramont

To my daughter, Tiana:

You persevered through challenges no child should ever face. When life knocked you off your feet, you found the courage to rise again, soft-hearted, strong-willed, and still choosing empathy in a world that didn't always show it to you. Your compassion is your superpower, and watching you grow into the woman you are has been the greatest chapter of any book I have ever written or ever will write. Being your mom is my life's most beautiful story.

To my grandson, Beckett:

You have just arrived in this world, and I welcome you with loving arms. Long after Grandma Koko is gone, I hope these words remind you where you came from. Lead with kindness. Chase every dream with joy and fire. Know that those that love you worked hard to build a life that makes your journey a little easier. And when it's your turn—because it will be—leave things better for the ones who come after you. That is how our family moves forward. That is how we build a legacy worthy of your future.

To my parents who raised me right,
my husband who raises my spirits,
and the women who raise each other up every day.

Contents

Introduction

♫ Somewhere Over the Rainbow ♫

It was one of those sun-soaked, blissfully perfect afternoons on the island of Kauai, the kind where the sun kisses your skin just right and leaves you glowing with that golden, goddess-like tan. I know, I know ... too much sun can cause wrinkles. But in that moment? I didn't care. I was soaking up every bit of Vitamin D and living my best beach life.

That morning, we'd been out surfing just behind the vacation rental condo we had booked for the final leg of our Hawaiian adventure. Well ... attempting to surf. I was mostly flailing around in the waves, catching a few short-lived rides and doing my best not to face-plant too hard. Surfing doesn't come naturally to me—turns out growing up landlocked in Georgia doesn't exactly prepare you for wave-riding. Add in my almost non-existent flexibility (I've tried yoga, Pilates ... the struggle is real), and I probably looked like a baby flamingo trying to stand on a yoga ball.

Still, I was trying, and that counted for something.

My daughter, Kiki, had already given up after some coral reef carnage. Kiki declared surfing "dumb" and was done for the day. Meanwhile, I sat on my board watching people of all ages glide gracefully across the water, making it look like they were born with fins. It was humbling, hilarious, and oddly motivating.

My husband paddled up beside me. “Let’s grab some lunch,” he suggested after another attempt left me swallowing saltwater. He was not doing much better, which made me feel a little better, but not in a mean way. He’s basically an all-American athlete, good at *everything*, so watching him struggle softened my bruised ego.

We wandered into a chill beach café—driftwood tables, tiki hut vibes, palm trees swaying, and Common Kings playing over the speakers. I don’t remember exactly what we ate, but I *do* remember how fresh and flavorful it was. We dug our toes into the sand, watching the pros surf while swapping wipeout stories.

Then the radio DJ casually dropped a bomb: Bethany Hamilton, my all-time favorite surfer, had just been spotted at Hanalei Bay. My jaw dropped.

“Alright, let’s load up,” my husband said, reading my face perfectly. “Mom wants to go surf with Bethany Hamilton.”

God, I love that man.

We piled into our comically small rental car, surfboards awkwardly shoved through the windows, and hit the road in search of my surf icon. Kiki was not thrilled having to duck under the boards on the winding road, but I was on cloud nine. This trip was already unforgettable-and about to get better.

But before I dive further into paradise, let me rewind two weeks.

Before Kauai, I had been on a quick Florida getaway with some coworkers. While they planned to spend Tuesday soaking up sun, I had other plans: a foreclosure auction was going live online, and there was a property I had my eye on.

The morning of the auction, while everyone else headed beachside with coolers and sunscreen, I was deep into spreadsheets, Google Maps, and comps. That certainly may not sound as fun as laying on the beach, but I knew the value of what I was doing. You see, by then I understood that sometimes you have to sacrifice to reach a goal. I knew that's what it takes to build wealth. That's the Boss Lady Investor mindset. It's the principle I live by: *Don't give up what you want most for what you want now.* (Thanks, Richard G. Scott.)

Unfortunately, I was outbid within three minutes of the auction starting. My mood sank as fast as my oat milk coffee. Disappointed, I was about to grab my beach bag and join the girls on the beach, when another foreclosure popped up on the auction website: a two-bedroom, one-bath home just two blocks from the beach. The bidding started at $60,000.

No time to tour. No photos. No info, just the address. But where else in the United States could you buy a house two blocks from the beach for $60,000? My inner voice spoke, *Go for it!*

I placed the minimum bid.

No one else bid.

Gulp.

Just like that, I became the proud (and slightly terrified) owner of a beachside house I knew almost nothing about. And because it was a foreclosure auction, I needed to come up with the cash within twenty-four hours. But here's where the magic of preparation comes in. Months before our girls trip, I had secured a HELOC (Home Equity Line of Credit) for moments exactly like this. When opportunity knocked, I was ready to answer the door.

Was I nervous? Of course. My husband was working overseas and had no idea I had just bought a house I didn't really know much of anything about besides the address. I hadn't seen the property. I didn't have a plan. But I *did* have the confidence to move forward. And that is what separates dreamers from doers.

I called my realtor and my contractor. "Meet me at the property."

When we arrived at the house, let's just say it had ... potential. A car with no wheels sat in the driveway. A broken-down boat in the yard. The inside? You could call it "hoarder-chic" if you're a cup-half-full kinda gal. And just to make things interesting, the former owner was still there.

But, get this, he was *helpful*. He gave us a full tour, admitted he couldn't maintain the payments, and handed me the key himself. No drama. No nightmare. Just a man ready for a new chapter, and a woman stepping into hers.

The Zillow data had the home showing as being 816 square feet, two bedrooms and one bathroom. Turns out there was an un-permitted addition, which wasn't calculated in the online info that, when added in, made the house a full three bedrooms, two bathrooms and 1,400 square feet.

Unpermitted addition—sounds scary, right? I was a little worried, too.

After a call to the city that took a whopping fifteen minutes of my time and a follow up email, I got the info I needed to close out the permit. There was a permit that *had been* filed, it was just never paid for, so I simply needed to pay. The cost to legalize it? A mere **sixty-eight dollars.** Jackpot!

All-in, I bought the house for just over $60,000. My contractor estimated the renovation costs at approximately $50,000. He and my realtor agreed it would make a great flip, but renovation work couldn't start for a month because of scheduling.

"Just list it," I told my realtor. "Let's see what happens. I'll deal with it when I get back from Hawaii."

So, a few weeks later, there we were in Hawaii, with Kiki crouched down in the backseat and my hubby expertly maneuvering the twists and turns of Kauai to get me to my favorite surf athlete, when my phone rang. My realtor said, "We received a cash offer. $112,000. No inspections. Can close in five days."

I smiled. "We'll take it."

Could I have renovated and made more money? Maybe. But I also could've opened a financial can of worms. Instead, I walked away with over $50,000 in profit in under two weeks, with almost zero effort.

And that? That was a Boss Lady Investor style win.

To add to that, when we got home, there was a lifted 4x4 Jeep sitting in our driveway—the one we had been eyeing because it was a crazy good deal but hadn't pulled the trigger on before the trip. Now? We had wired the cash to the seller from Hawaii, and he delivered it to our house before we returned. From that flip. From that moment of boldness.

No, I didn't get to surf with Bethany Hamilton that day. But I *did* learn something even better:

Real estate investing works.

How did I get here?

To the place where I can bid on a foreclosure without a knot in my stomach?

Where I knew to have a HELOC in place so I'm ready the moment a deal pops up?

Where I can wire sixty grand while my husband is overseas, without asking anyone's permission?

It didn't start with a trust fund, formal training, or even a mentor. I began with zero experience, no safety net, and a heart full of doubt ... and in less than a decade, built a multi-million-dollar portfolio.

For me, the journey started years before that Hawaii trip. It was messy, imperfect, and definitely not overnight. In the pages ahead, I'll walk you through the steps I took so you can create your own version of this story.

Here's what I need every Boss Lady to remember: *Where you start has nothing to do with how far you can go.*

You might be at the top of your career or at rock bottom. It doesn't matter if you're single, divorced, in a rough marriage, or blissfully partnered—your relationship status does **not** define your potential. Real estate doesn't care about your ring finger. Like some of you, there have been times when I have cried myself to sleep, wondering if I'd ever climb out of my financial traps or become worthy of love.

Your lowest point is not the end of your story; in fact, it's often the birthplace of your strongest chapters.

Success, whether in real estate or life, isn't about perfect timing or a flawless plan. It's about showing up when it's uncomfortable, staying focused when it's messy, and trusting that steady action with the right intentions will carry you forward. And I learned something powerful through every late night and every hard lesson: if you commit, work hard, and move forward with a clear purpose, you will succeed.

Your power comes from your decisions, your actions, and your belief that the future belongs to you.

The tools are already inside you. All you need is the mindset to use them.

Chapter 1
THE BOSS LADY MINDSET

It's Your Time to ♫ Roar ♫

Hey There, Boss Lady!

Congratulations! You have decided to take control of your financial future, to learn something that most people are too intimidated to even Google, and to bet on *yourself*.

You picked up a book on real estate investing. That decision alone puts you in rare *but exceptional* company.

Welcome to becoming part of a growing force of women who are stepping into wealth-building, smashing outdated ceilings, and paving the way for others to rise.

Learning about finances is not that different from starting a workout regimen. When women decide to get in shape, we like to set goals: "I'm going to start jogging, and by spring I will run a 5k." We start training, walking, jogging a little, then jogging more until we reach the day of the race. For some of us, we find that we enjoy fitness and see that it improves our quality of life, so we go even further with it. That first small step can lead to 10k's, half-marathons, marathons, maybe even an Ironman.

Regardless of where you end up in your journey, you are improving yourself physically *and* mentally.

Money works the same way. It's okay to be nervous about getting started. I've been jogging for thirty years and *still* come up with excuses in my head to skip. You name it, I've thought it: *My knees hurt. I have work to do. I don't have time.*

I'll be honest, there are still days when the last thing I want to do is learn something new about money. But just like fitness, building financial strength requires a goal that keeps you moving forward. Some days the workouts feel effortless; other days every step is a grind. It's the same with finances. Some women start small, like running their first 5K, and then keep training until they're marathon investors. Others reach a comfortable milestone and decide that's enough. And yes, some never make it to that first race, just as some never reach their financial goals.

But crossing that initial finish line is only the beginning. Like physical fitness, financial fitness will fade if you stop training. The minute you quit learning and applying new tools, your money muscles stop growing. Stay curious, keep pushing, and your financial education will keep paying you back long after the first victory lap.

The proverbial ball is in your court.

You have the choice.

And you, Boss Lady, are putting in the work just by picking up this book. *Cheers!*

You are now part of a league of women that are moving the needle for all women.

This book isn't just about real estate investing; it's about transformation. It's about shifting your mindset from "*Can I really do this?* to "*Watch me.*" It's about building a life of financial freedom and fearlessly knowing that you can generate lasting wealth—not just for yourself, but for your family, your community, and for every woman watching you lead by example.

You are a leader, or at least becoming one. Own it and be proud.

Maybe you picked up this book because you have dreams of owning a long-term rental to create an additional income stream. Perhaps you want to learn how to invest in a home in a beautiful locale that you will retire in one day. Or maybe you are dreaming of building an empire of properties across the country. Possibly, like me, your dreams include everything from having the added monthly income, to creating a fabulous lifestyle, to having a beach house, ski lodge and villa in Italy.

No matter what shape they take, your dreams are perfect. Having aspirations is what makes life exciting. Setting goals with creativity and intention, nourishes your brain *and* your heart.

One of our many gifts as women is that we understand a home is so much more than walls and a roof. A home is a castle. It's where memories are made, where we retreat for safety, where children grow and laughter echoes. Some homes will hold vacation magic, others will welcome you after a long day, and some may cradle you through tears in the middle of a messy divorce. One will even be the place where you savor your final, joyful years.

Our sensitivity and emotion are superpowers, my friend. Use them. They guide us toward wise investments and help us recognize when a property is more than just a deal. Our brains and our hearts were designed to work together, so let them.

And this is only the beginning. We have so many more superpowers to uncover. Whatever your dream may be, it's valid, it's powerful, and it starts right here. You don't have to know every step yet; you only need the courage to take the first one. And you've already done that.

You are not alone in this journey. Let's build something legendary.

This book was created to give women the guidance, support, and shortcuts that are so often missing when starting the journey into real estate investing. Many people begin without a mentor or roadmap, facing unnecessary struggles and setbacks. These pages are designed to change that, to help women reach their goals faster, with more clarity, and with less stress along the way.

Like you, when I first became interested in real estate investing, I was hungry to learn. *I still am.* Yet it seemed like many of the books I picked up (or listened to) had good info but were frankly boring. It felt like the tone, the examples, the assumptions ... it all felt just a little disconnected. I kept thinking, *Where are the women in this story? Where are the moms, the single ladies, the corporate dropouts and ladder climbers, the dreamers, the hustlers, the former strippers, the boss babes balancing it all?*

Writing my first book, *Becoming a Boss Lady Investor,* felt a lot like buying my first designer handbag—it carried all the essentials I needed to start my financial journey. That book was written for beginner-me, the woman who had no clue where to start. It held the basics: how to budget, how to dip into the stock market, how to make sense of retirement plans, and, most importantly, how to stop treating money like it was some mysterious, off-limits secret. I wrote it because I desperately needed it, and I knew other women did too. At the time, there wasn't a single book that spoke to women like me, without mansplaining, without boredom, and without judgment.

Fast forward a few years (and a few properties later), and I had a major realization: real estate wasn't just another accessory, it was my *statement piece*. The investment that pulled the whole look together. Real estate is what catapulted me from financially stable to building true generational wealth. It's what moved me into the top 2% of wealth holders in the United States. And I'll be real with you; I've got my sights on the top 1%. I'm not there yet ... but I'm on my way.

This book is for the women that want to take their investment knowledge to the next level. It's not for everyone. Real estate investing can be fun, but the reason everyone isn't doing it is because *it's not easy*.

Nothing worthwhile is.

The good news is, you *will* learn if you take the time to educate yourself, practice and keep growing. That's the secret sauce.

Here's another secret: Women tend to worry about perceived "greed," often hiding their desire to make money. But here's the scoop: There are people with money that do great things for the world, and people that don't. There are people with no money that do great things for the world, and people that don't. For me, I have been able to do better when I am financially strong than when I am not. If that is greed, then so be it. Don't apologize. You can do great things for a lot of people when you are financially strong.

My hope is that the pages ahead make real estate investing not just accessible, but a whole lot more fun for us ladies. The great news? It *is* fun and the stats prove it's one of our favorite ways to build wealth. Even better, we're damn good at it! This book isn't just about crunching numbers (though we'll cover that too); it's written to speak to you as a real woman living a real life. No fluff. No BS. Just straight talk and strategies that work.

Worried that you don't have enough money to start investing? Good news, real estate investing isn't just for the wealthy and the well-connected. It's for any woman who is ready to take control of her time, her money, and her legacy. It's for the woman who wants to stop waiting for permission and start building wealth on her own terms.

I get asked, why specifically for women? Here's my answer through an analogy. When a woman picks up a new sport, she usually learns best by practicing with other women. Our bodies move differently than a man's; our strengths develop in unique ways, and we feel more evenly matched. That shared experience helps us build confidence, master the fundamentals, and grow comfortable working alongside one another.

Sure, we can invest with men, just like we can play mixed doubles in tennis. But too often, I see women get anxious or second-guess themselves when it feels like we've stumbled into a boys' club. The jargon, the egos, and the strategies that don't resonate with us can make our eyes glaze over. No wonder so many women feel overwhelmed or discouraged before even making their first move.

This is for us, for women learning, growing, and investing together. It's about seeing examples that look like us. About building wealth without shame, fear, or feeling like we have to "man up". It's time to play the investing game on our own terms with a tribe of badass women by our side, cheering every win and learning from every loss.

My message to you is simple: You belong here. And I'm going to show you exactly how to get started.

The Past is Prologue

Women in Real Estate Investing
♫ Man, I Feel Like a Woman ♫

To the women that came before us and paved the way for our chapter, *Thank you.* We have made significant strides, but still, while women dominate the residential sales side of real estate, making up over 65% of all REALTORS®, their presence as active real estate investors has historically lagged. In the U.S., only about 30 to 32% of real estate investors are women. But that number is rising fast.

More women are stepping into the investing arena with purpose and power. In fact, single women are now the fastest growing group of homebuyers, often outpacing single men in their pursuit of homeownership and investment properties. Globally, surveys show that more than 70% of women now consider real estate their preferred investment class, up from 65% just a few years ago.

What's more, when women do invest, they often outperform men. A 2021 study by the Boston Consulting Group found that women-led real estate investment funds deliver returns up to 1.5 times higher than those managed by men.

Did you see that I said 1.5 times higher? Want to know what that *actually* means? Let's break it down. If a male-led real estate fund earns a 10% return, and a woman-led fund earns 1.5 times higher, that means the woman-led fund is bringing in 15%.

So, if both funds invested $100,000, the men would earn $10,000, but the women? They'd earn $15,000.

That's an extra $5,000 just from smarter strategy, better decision-making, and a different perspective. It's not about luck or emotion, it's about performance. And numbers like that prove what we already know: when women invest, we *crush it.*

Despite the growing momentum, women still face unique barriers—access to capital, education gaps, and a male-dominated investing culture. But this is also where opportunity lives. With only a third of the investing field currently made up of women, there's massive room for growth. As more women claim their seat at the table, they're not just changing their own financial futures—they're transforming the landscape of real estate investing.

Boss Lady Meets Backstage Pass
♬ *Respect* ♬

I love celebrating badass women who are paving the road ahead. Each chapter in this book is more than just a lesson in real estate investing—it's a tribute to the fierce, fabulous women who've unapologetically owned the stage, smashed the mold, and rewritten the rules.

I wanted to make the book fun, and I love music, so you'll find references to songstresses you may love (or not) along the journey. These ladies smashed the mold in their own worlds. From the resilience of TayTay to the reinvention power of the Material Girl, these rockstar icons help inspire my mindset behind every move I make in real estate (and are often playing in my earbuds as I make these major financial moves).

Whether you're flipping houses or buying your first rental, you'll find a little swagger, a little sparkle, and a whole lot of Boss Lady energy woven into every chapter. Building wealth should feel as powerful as belting out your favorite in the front row.

The Boss Lady Mindset

Every Woman Can be a
♬ *Girl on Fire* ♬

There is no prerequisite to financial success: that's right, no trust fund, rich husband, or degree in finance needed to build serious wealth. What you do need are the guts to go after what you want, the smarts to learn the game, and the fire to keep showing up, even when it's hard, even when it's scary, even when no one's cheering you on. Become enchanted by yourself. Real estate changed my life, and if you're holding this book, I have a feeling it's about to change yours too.

What starts as curiosity can quickly grow into something bigger, an obsession, in the best way. And unlike falling for a bad boy, diving headfirst into this kind of relationship can lead to a life that feels a whole lot like a fairy tale. You'll find yourself soaking up knowledge everywhere you can—podcasts on your commute, blogs late into the night, and books that offer even a sliver of insight. You're not just daydreaming about a different future; you're building it, brick by brick, deal by deal. And the best part? You're already on that path.

I want to give you the tools to get started, and then, if you want to take it further from there, that's up to you. I will try not to give you information overload or bore you with big words or fancy formulas that you will likely never use. We are going to go over the basics, but much of your learning will come from doing. I'm going to try to help you avoid mistakes, save money and get there faster. However, *you* still must do the work. This book is the start of your journey, but *you* must keep the motivation to keep climbing the mountains.

♫ *Love (and Mindset) is a Battlefield* ♫

Whether you picked up this book with big dreams or just a little curiosity, you're in the right place.

I think you will find some great nuggets ahead. Maybe in the past you've felt the *"red"* (the frustration, the confusion, the fear) when it comes to investing. That's all normal. Investing can be intimidating, and those jitters are natural.

Babe, you don't have to know everything. You just have to get started.

You don't need to become the next Barbara Corcoran overnight. Even just one smart investment can help you:

- Create passive income
- Build generational wealth
- Diversify your financial portfolio, and
- Prove to yourself that you're a damn powerhouse

And if you *do* want to build a mini real estate empire?

Guess what? You'll find the roadmap in these pages to make that happen, too. You'll learn:

- How to evaluate deals with confidence
- Ways to fund your investments (even if your bank account says "not today")
- How to grow at your own pace without burning out
- And how to handle the inevitable bumps (or leaky toilets) along the way

No matter your goal, one property or one hundred, I want you to feel empowered, educated, and capable. I want you to stop sitting on the sidelines watching everyone else win at the wealth game. Whether you're tiptoeing into the shallow end or cannonballing off the deep side, you belong here.

Let's start seeing green and leave all those red flags behind.

My real estate empire didn't start with a glamorous investment portfolio. Not at all. It started in my early twenties, with a meltdown in Atlanta traffic.

In the next chapter I will share about how I had my "ah-ha" moment during a ladies' tennis trip, when sitting in my friend's aunt's beach house first sparked my curiosity about real estate investing. But finally *acting* on that spark came years later and in a far less glamorous setting.

But back to my meltdown. At the time, I was working in the stock market. On paper, it was everything I thought I wanted: a prestigious job, great pay, and a fast climb up the corporate ladder. By traditional measures, I should have been thrilled. Instead, I found myself stuck in gridlock traffic, inching toward a job I didn't love. On a "good" day, my commute was an hour. Most days, it was closer to two ... each way. I tried everything to make it tolerable: books on CD, music, license plate games, even commuter vans. Nothing worked. The grind was draining the life, and time, right out of me.

And the work itself? Cold-calling strangers, convincing them to buy whatever preferred stocks or mutual funds my firm was pushing that day. It felt transactional. Hollow. Truthfully? Icky. Don't get me wrong, I still believe in the stock market. I have a financial advisor for part of my portfolio, I dabble on Robinhood, and I absolutely believe in maxing out retirement accounts. But deep down, I couldn't ignore how uncomfortable I'd become with the system I was part of.

Here's the deal: the goal of major financial firms isn't to secure your future, it's to secure theirs.

And that's when it hit me: my sense of professional "success" was tied to something I had zero control over—the stock market. I could only feel "proud" of my work if the market happened to go my way and, therefore, my clients' way.

Even worse, I realized that my future was also tied to that same volatile system. If the market tanked, so could my entire retirement account. Us, the brokers, the ones selling the dream, would drive the luxury cars, wear the custom suits, and send our kids to private schools to project an image of money. All while marketing to our clients the importance of saving money. That felt wrong.

I don't doubt that many financial advisors *do* care about their clients. But I've also seen the structure up close, and that structure isn't designed to put the client first. It's designed to protect the firm.

I'm incredibly grateful for the education and experience I gained in that chapter of my life; however, I don't believe the stock market should be the only strategy for building wealth. In my opinion, I think it's the world's largest legal casino. Sure, regulatory agencies may exist, but that does not make it much safer than blackjack.

Don't believe me? Let's check out a few moments in stock market history.

Bernie Madoff pulled off the largest investment fraud in history: $65 billion. He targeted people in his own religious community, celebrities, and major institutions. And he was the *former chairman of the NASDAQ*.

Then there's Lehman Brothers, the fourth-largest investment bank in the U.S. They loaded up on toxic subprime mortgage debt and helped trigger the 2008 global financial meltdown. Their bankruptcy totaled more than $600 billion, the largest in history (and not one senior executive was ever prosecuted).

And don't even get me started on how male-dominated the entire industry still is. Leadership is overwhelmingly male, and the culture, though slowly shifting, remains built for them. Golf outings, late-night dealmaking, and "boys club" networking still dominates the backrooms where the big decisions are made.

Meanwhile, women like Martha Stewart, the first self-made female billionaire in the U.S., dip their toe into the boy's club and get nailed to the wall.

Contrary to popular belief, Martha was not convicted of insider trading. Her broker told her to sell a stock, and she did. What landed her in prison? Obstruction of justice, conspiracy, and making false statements. Her case became a spectacle, while executives at giant financial firms skated free after collapsing the economy.

If you haven't watched her documentary or read her book—do it. Martha is the definition of a Boss Lady Investor: resilient, sharp, and unshakably classy. She's proof that even when women *play the game*, we are often judged by a different set of rules. She also loves Snoop Dogg and so do I, so that puts her on an even higher pedestal for me, but I digress.

Back to my realization that my life was not what I wanted it to be.

There came that point—somewhere between the cold calls, the commission goals, and the insane traffic—when I realized just how unfulfilled I was. I was working in the stock market, surrounded by people who measured success in numbers, titles, and suits ... and depending on that world to fund my future. But deep down, I knew this couldn't be it.

This was my life. And if I wanted *all the things*—the freedom, the joy, the adventure—I'd have to figure out how to get there on my own terms. (After two divorces, you start to question how viable marriage is as a financial or emotional safety net). I was not willing to stake my future on someone else's decisions ever again.

Thinking Like a ♬ SheWolf ♬

Okay, let's get into your head. Many women I coach feel a little "not enough" at first. *"I don't know enough. I'm not handy. I don't have rich parents, I'm not married, or I don't have a big savings account."*

Girl, hush that voice.

Let me tell you, I've seen single moms, retirees, teachers, corporate queens, women from every walk of life absolutely CRUSH it in real estate. Not because they were born rich. But because they decided to try.

When you mess up? You learn. Trust me, I have stories that would curl your hair—like the time my bestie and I bought a triplex. After getting it fixed up and rented out, code enforcement cited us because the property was not, in fact, a triplex. Girl, I am a long-time real estate investor who has educated myself like crazy and I still messed up. Did I quit? Nope. I adjusted and made sure it didn't happen again. And now, I'm telling you about it in a book focused on making money in real estate. Mistakes can often be your best lessons. You simply have to be willing to learn the lesson and make changes the next time.

So, repeat after me: *I am a SheWolf/Lioness/Rockstar. I am capable. I am resourceful. I will figure it out. I will not be the anti-hero of my story.* There. Now you're ready.

The Lioness Inside

♬ *Unstoppable* ♬

Speaking of journeys, my absolute favorite place to visit on the planet is Africa. The rawness of the land, the people and the animals touch the deepest parts of my soul. I love the beauty of the giraffes, the strange noises of the hippos, and even the weird hyenas that make me smile.

I love every moment when I am on the "continent." But the moment that touched the deepest, most primal part of me, was during an early morning safari in Sabi Sands, South Africa. We were sipping coffee while overlooking a small creek, enjoying the start to another day. In the golden light of dawn, the savanna was still: zebras grazing quietly, antelope ears flicking at the breeze. Suddenly, a deep, rolling sound cut through the silence: the roar of a lioness.

Her call wasn't just noise: it was a declaration. She wasn't the largest in the pride, nor the one with the heavy mane, but her roar carried just as far, echoing nearly five miles across the plains. For her cubs, it was reassurance: *Mama's here.* For rival predators, it was a warning: *Stay away.* And for the pride, it was unity: *We hunt, we protect, we thrive, together.*

Unlike the roar of a male lion, often used to mark territory, the lioness's roar is rooted in protection and connection. It is the sound of leadership, of courage, of fierce love.

That morning on the savanna, her roar reminded everyone within earshot of a simple truth: a lioness doesn't need to be seen to be felt—her power speaks for her.

It's time for you to roar!

Chapter 2
GET READY TO ROCK 'N ROLL

♪ *Look What You Made Me Do* ♪

If you've read *Becoming a Boss Lady Investor*, you already know a bit of my story. If you're new here: *Welcome*. I'll share parts of my journey along the way to give you a laugh, answer questions, and maybe spark ideas. But let's be clear: this isn't really about me; it's about you.

So, what made you pick up this book? What do you hope to gain from real estate investing? What's your *WHY*—the reason you're dedicating your precious time to learn and grow? It's a question worth asking yourself often, because the answer changes as life does. My *WHY* at sixteen looked very different from my *WHY* at twenty-six, thirty-six, or forty-six. In this chapter of your life, what's yours?

Discover Your *WHY*

Maybe you're craving more free time. Maybe you're stuck in a job that drains you, or one that will never lead to the financial freedom you deserve. Maybe you're tired of that pit in your stomach when bills are due. Or maybe you're dreaming of a side hustle that could pay for the extras: the girls' trips, the upgraded house, the little luxuries. Maybe you simply want the chance to be rich, and there's nothing wrong with saying that out loud.

I'll admit it. I love expensive things—traveling the world, eating incredible food, chasing adrenaline with whitewater rafting, skydiving, and safaris in Africa. Those things cost money, so I make sure I have plenty of it, and I have zero shame in saying that. If you think it's taboo to want wealth, stop right here. Boss Ladies don't have time for that nonsense.

Whatever drives you, knowing your *WHY* matters. Because here's the truth: tough times will come. And when they do, that *WHY* will be the thing that pushes you through.

It took me a long time—and a lot of soul searching—to uncover mine. For years, I thought my *WHY* was to travel. But the deeper I dug, the more I realized it was so much bigger.

Acknowledging
♬ *Our Song* ♬

At my core, I've always been a wild child—a free spirit who craves freedom in every sense of the word.

Freedom to travel the world and learn new languages.

Freedom to give both time and money to causes I care about.

Freedom to be a present mom or grandma.

Freedom to run for office and create meaningful change.

Freedom to build things that light up my soul.

Freedom to work out at noon, to learn to dance just because it's fun, to speak my truth, and to only stand behind things I truly believe in.

And most of all? Financial freedom, the kind that doesn't depend on a man, a job, or anything that could crumble beneath me.

That realization was my turning point. I knew I had to build something real, something that aligned with who I was and what I wanted out of life. For me, that "something" became real estate. And once I claimed that freedom, I made it my mission to help other women claim theirs too.

My journey has been full of twists, setbacks, breakthroughs, and hard-won lessons, and I know yours has too. Every woman has her own path that led her here, to this moment.

So, let me ask you again: What's your purpose? Your goal? Your *WHY*?

What brought you to this moment, the one where you're ready to think differently, act boldly, and step out of the box you've been living in? What made you say, *I want more*? Why did you grab this book and decide to explore real estate investing?

Take a second and choose one word that defines your *WHY*. Write it down. Circle it. Doodle it in the margins. Make it yours. And then hang on to it because that word will be your anchor when things get tough (and they will).

There will be days when you doubt yourself. When deals fall apart. When it feels like you're clawing through dirt with your bare hands and the dream looks far away. But that's part of the process. Nothing worth having comes easy.

The journey takes time, grit, and consistency. And let's be real, don't go quitting your job tomorrow just because you've decided to become an investor. Financial freedom isn't a magic switch. But if you stick with it, keep showing up, and keep your *WHY* close, you'll be amazed at how far you can go.

For most of us, it takes years of consistent effort before you can go full-time into real estate, if that's even your goal. Some will move faster, others slower. You do you. There's no one-size-fits-all path.

But if you stick with it? You will likely get to the point where you're living off your investments, not living to work.

And that to me, my friend, is freedom. Freedom is my *WHY*.

I like to think of real estate investing like the rise of Taylor Swift. She didn't become a global icon overnight. She started young, stayed consistent, took creative control, pivoted when necessary, and wasn't afraid to take bold risks. When she wasn't "country" enough for country music or "pop" enough for pop, she said, "hold my beer". Then she went on to become one of the best-selling artists of all time in both genres. Real estate can be the same: you start small, maybe with a fixer-upper or house hack, stay consistent with your strategy, learn as you go, adapt when the market shifts, and keep your long-term vision clear. Just like Taylor built an empire one song, one tour, and one fearless decision at a time, you can build wealth one property, one deal, and one bold move at a time.

Alright, powerhouses, take a deep breath, do a little shoulder roll, maybe add in a downward dog and get ready. Because by the end of this chapter, you'll not only *believe* you can be a real estate investor, but you'll also have a plan to get moving.

Pick Your Passion, Then Make it a ♫ Love Story ♫

Let me share an example. I love vacation rentals. I've hosted everyone from honeymooners to rowdy bachelorette parties (oh, the stories ...). Because *I love it*, I learn the market inside-out, decorate vacation homes like a boss, and give my guests experiences they rave about online. Because *I love it*, I love spending time working on my vacation rental portfolio.

My friend Kara? She could not care less about Airbnb or VRBO. She prefers long-term rentals—clean, quiet families, year-long leases, minimal fuss. That's her jam.

MIC DROP MOMENT

You can dabble, but mastery makes money.

Your homework: answer these questions honestly to help you find where your passion may be in real estate investing.

- What excites you about real estate investing?
- Do you like design and renovations? Or do you prefer turnkey?
- Do you want monthly rent checks or big paydays a few times a year? Or both?

Come up with some questions of your own, too. Then compare your answers to the real estate strategies you learn in this book to create a path that is in-line with who you are. Write down your vibe. Knowing your natural energy helps you pick your strategy.

> **ROCKSTAR TIP**
> Find your vibe. Use it to chart your personal roadmap to real estate success.

For me, I love design work. Risk excites me; it makes my heart beat faster and I feel alive. It's no surprise that a lot of my portfolio consists of vacation rental investments which are notoriously more volatile. However, I also have a side of me that knows stability leads to long term growth, so I marry my vacation rentals with a portfolio of long-term rentals to provide diversification. But that's just me. What excites you yet also allows you to sleep at night?

Set Smart Goals: Live Your ♫ Wildest Dreams ♫

Let's set the stage with some honest-to-goodness goal setting. Not the Pinterest-perfect, dreamy stuff. Real, gritty, powerful goal setting that puts your dreams on paper.

Grab your pen, Boss Lady. Write it down. Say it out loud. Text your bestie. Accountability and visibility are secret ingredients to success.

You wouldn't start a road trip without a destination. Same for investing.

My first goals looked like this:

- Cash flow $3,000/month in passive income
- Own 5 rental properties
- Buy a vacation rental
- Be debt-free by age 40

- Have $1 million in retirement assets by age 55

My Current Goals? Oh, they've grown:

- Cash flow $50,000/month
- Sell one property a year for $300k+ profit
- Own vacation homes in three favorite travel destinations
- Stay completely debt-free
- Mentor 50 women into their first investment property each year

Let me be clear: this journey isn't about becoming a landlord. It's about becoming the architect of your life. It's about options. Freedom. Power. Legacy.

And while we're being real, let's talk about fear. Because it's going to rear its ugly head. That nervous energy? That pit in your stomach when you think about buying your first property. It's normal. But you've done scary things before, haven't you?

You've left a toxic job. You've navigated messy relationships. You've built a career, raised kids, managed chaos.

Real estate? You've got this.

No one starts as an expert. The goal is to start. And to keep going.

By now, I hope you have a list of reasons why you want to build wealth through real estate. Not my reasons. Yours. These will carry you through the hard days. Through the deals that fall through. Through the surprise repairs, the messy tenants, the days when your dreams feel far away.

Here are a few common WHYs I hear from women I mentor:

- I want freedom to travel.
- I never want to rely on one job or one person again.
- I want to create generational wealth.
- I want to retire early.
- I want to fund a nonprofit or a cause that matters to me.
- I want to get out of the rat race.

Once you understand your "why", it's time to set goals. Goals are different from your WHY because goals are measurable. Here are some examples of goals I have seen in the real estate investing world:

- Create passive income (insert your monthly dollar amount) through rental properties.
- Replace 9-5 income with real estate cash flow.
- Acquire $1 million in real estate assets by age __ (or within _ years).
- Eliminate debt using profits from rentals or property flips.
- Purchase your first investment property within 12 months.
- Expand to 5 properties (or 10 doors) by a target year.
- Add a beachfront or vacation rental to your portfolio with _ years.
- Buy one property per year for the next decade.
- Grow into a portfolio worth $5 million in assets.

What are your goals? Please don't skimp on this, and don't tell yourself your goal is to "get started in real estate investing." Pick something precise and measurable. Don't be afraid to state numbers: dollar amounts, time frames, number of units and don't be afraid to scale your goals as you gain experience and success. My first goal was five rental properties. Once I understood the game better and had those five doors, I made even bigger goals.

Write yours down. Tell a friend. Put them on your bathroom mirror. Accountability makes dreams real.

Whether you're starting in your 20s or 60s, whether you've got $5,000 or $500,000, I want you to feel this truth deep in your soul.

You. Can. Do. This.

Grab your coffee. Open your notebook.

Let's build something that lasts.

Know Your Options

Investment Strategies, Know Them
♫ All Too Well ♫

Let's unpack this. Real estate is a massive world with countless ways to play. So, let's get clear about options out there.

There are many ways I have seen Boss Ladies use real estate to enhance or grow their portfolio. Some techniques are relatively easy, while others are quite complex. No book can cover every style of investing, and this one will focus on a specific few that I find relatively easy ways to get started, but I do want to share a few others that you will want to be aware of on your journey:

Wholesaling. Find great deals, sell the contract to another investor, collect a fee. (No owning, no repairs). I have purchased several incredible deals from wholesalers; however,

I am not an expert on *being* the wholesaler. There are many people that make great money doing this, but it takes a tremendous amount of hustle. It's not my cup of tea, but there are investors that love doing it. If you want to learn more about wholesaling, check out these books:

The Real Estate Wholesaling Bible, by Than Merrill
The Beginners Guide to Wholesaling Real Estate, by Jeff Leighton

Real Estate Investment Trusts (REITs). Buy shares in big real estate projects without owning actual properties. These are typically done through brokerage accounts. To learn more about REITS, reach out to your financial advisor or consider exchange-traded funds.

Syndication. Another creative way to invest in real estate, especially if you want to be involved without managing tenants or fixing leaky faucets, is through real estate syndication. This is where a group of investors pool their money to buy a property that would be tough to purchase solo, like an apartment complex or commercial space. Usually, there's a "sponsor" or lead investor who finds and manages the deal, while the others invest passively and share in the profits. It's a great way to diversify your portfolio and build wealth without taking on all the day-to-day work yourself. If this piques your interest, there are entire books and podcasts dedicated to syndications that can help you dive deeper into this strategy.

All of these are great options for investment. We are not going to cover them all though. In this book, we're going to focus on a few proven winners.

Long-Term Rentals. We will start here because it's the most common and often the easiest entry point for new investors. Whether a single-family home, a condo, or a small duplex, long-term rentals provide consistent monthly income and are relatively easy to manage. (Chapter 3)

BRRRR Method. Buy, Rehab, Rent, Refinance, Repeat. Recycle your money and grow fast. We are going to deep dive into this in the next chapter. This is my go-to style of investing, and many real estate investing pros do the same. We touch on this in multiple chapters as it can be used in various scenarios. It's also the formula I am most familiar with and have seen many Boss Ladies benefit from so we will go into detail on this topic.

House Hacking. Buy a duplex, live in one unit, rent the other. Boom, your mortgage is covered (or at least some of it). Seems easy enough, right? We'll explore the benefits (and costs) of this option.

Vacation Rentals. This is where we dive into short-term rentals, like Airbnb and VRBO properties. These can be high reward, but they come with more work, higher turnover, and unique challenges. The upside? If done well, they can generate significantly more cash flow than long-term rentals. Plus, you can enjoy them on your own vacations most of the time. (Chapter 4)

Fix-and-Flips. Not for the faint of heart, flipping requires capital, connections, and a tolerance for risk. But it can also be highly profitable and incredibly satisfying when you take a rundown property and turn it into someone's dream home—and make a solid profit doing it. (Chapter 5)

Multi-Family Properties. We'll cover multi-family properties like duplexes, triplexes, fourplexes, and small apartment buildings. While most Boss Lady Investors may not head down this path right away, it's important to understand the basics. Multi-unit investing plays a big role in wealth building, and if it piques your interest, there's a plethora of resources out there to help you dive deeper when you're ready. (Chapter 6)

And of course, the big question in real estate investing is always, how will I pay for it? So, we will be discussing:

Funding Your Deals. None of this happens without money. Whether you're working with traditional lenders, creative financing, partnerships, or using equity in your own home, we'll break down the most common (and practical) ways to fund your real estate investments—even if you're starting with limited capital. (Chapters 7 and 8)

Don't worry, I'll unpack each one like a pro stylist unpacking designer bags at a trunk show.

Funding Like a
♬ Fearless ♬ Boss

This is the juicy part. Let's talk money. One of the biggest hurdles for most new investors? Funding. So yes, we'll break down how to pay for this dream life.

No sugar coating it, real estate isn't free. But it IS doable. And the more options you understand, the more empowered you become. Here are some options we will discuss, I'm sure there are more out there, and you can certainly keep educating yourself. (Follow me on Instagram *@thebossladyinvestor* and share any interesting funding options you find!)

For now, the options we will cover in this book (Chapters 7 and 8) are:

Cash. Obvious but not always realistic.

Conventional Loans. Best rates, 20–25% down for investment property.

FHA/VA Loans. Live in the property a year, then rent it out (house hack!).

HELOC. Use equity in your home. Smart if you have discipline.

Seller Financing. The seller holds the note for you.

"Subject To" Deals. You take over the sellers payments

DSCR Loans. Income-based instead of credit-based.

Private Money. Borrowing dough from your friends.

Hard Money. Short-term loan for flips. High interest, but quick.

Partnerships. Pool resources with a trusted friend or family member.

Self-Directed IRA. Riskier, but can supercharge your retirement growth.

1031 Exchange. Defers taxes and makes money available for your next property purchase.

Let's face it, most of us weren't taught this in school. They didn't offer "Wealth Building 101" in high school, and that's exactly why this book exists. I want to fill in the gaps, hand you the blueprint, and cheer you on as you build your empire.

Once you have a good understanding of how various types of funding work, pick what suits your risk tolerance and timeline. I did this completely wrong when I first got started, but that's great news for you because now you can learn from my mistakes. We are *all* going to make mistakes along the way, so get the best education you can and then be ready to forgive yourself as needed when things happen. Because that's life.

Getting Stuck in
♫ *Blank Space* ♫

Analysis paralysis is real. I've seen women spend YEARS "learning" but never doing. Don't be her.

> **MIC DROP MOMENT**
>
> Done is better than perfect.
>
> - *Brené Brown*

Done is better than perfect. The amazing Boss Lady Brené Brown emphasizes that striving for perfection often stops us from starting or *finishing* the things that matter. One of her most powerful metaphors about this comes from *The Gifts of Imperfection*, where she writes:

> *Perfectionism is a twenty-ton shield that we lug around thinking it will protect us when, in fact, it's the thing that's really preventing us from taking flight.*

In other words: the quest to be perfect, whether in our work, our relationships, or our self-presentation, often acts as a barrier to progress and connection. Ironically, that "shield" meant to safeguard us weighs us down.

Yes, learn the basics. But then, get out there:

- Drive neighborhoods.
- Talk to local agents.
- Go to open houses (bring a friend and make a day of it!).
- Join investor meetups or online groups.

ROCKSTAR TIP

Keep a notebook in your car. Notice patterns: homes for sale, new construction, rentals.

This boots-on-the-ground research is gold. You'll learn which neighborhoods have good schools, which streets flood, where values are rising, and what tenants want.

Let me repeat—I have seen women spend YEARS "learning," inviting me to have coffee to "pick my brain" and talking about "one day when they are ready." I've stopped accepting coffee invites at this point because I'm not wasting my precious time on someone else's fantasy. If you are committed to this, you need to move forward with action and stop procrastinating.

Don't be the girl that looks back and wishes she had. Don't be her.

Before You Start

First Things First

Are You Ready for It?

Let's keep it real. If you're reading this, I already know you're a doer. A woman who doesn't just talk about dreams, she chases them. There will be millions of people that dream about investing, building wealth and growing their futures, but you are one of the few that will actually do it. You are a rockstar. But hear me: real estate investing is not just about buying cute houses and collecting checks. It is a business. A real one.

Before you spend a penny, promise me you have your financial ducks in a row:

A healthy emergency fund. You've probably heard that three to six months' worth of current expenses stashed in cash is a healthy emergency fund. I happen to agree. However, *know thyself*. If having a year's worth of savings helps you sleep better at night, then save up, sister. The point is that you shouldn't start investing until you know that you are in a safe place to do so.

No high-interest debt dragging you down. Pay off those credit cards, mama! Investors don't carry monthly credit card balances and make minimum payments. That's not to say we don't use credit cards. I use them for most of my daily purchases because I want the benefits they offer—travel perks, Amazon credits and more. But, and this is a HUGE but, I pay them off in full every single month. Most cards have interest rates in the high teens, twenties or even higher. You're not going to get rich or build wealth if your everyday purchases are costing you 20% more than market value due to credit card interest.

A basic budget that you follow (most days!). This doesn't mean you have to follow it to the penny; few people are *that* disciplined—me included. But create something that works for you. For example, when I get a real estate commission check, I split it like this:

- 1/3 towards an investment (that could be a stock purchase, paying towards a mortgage on a property I

own or putting money into a CD, depending on the market and my situation at that moment).
- 1/3 to my checking account.
- 1/3 to something fun. For me that could mean new golf clubs or paying even more towards a mortgage on a property I own. I happen to think paying off debt is fun, and I like getting closer to my goals faster.

That is my style of budgeting.

If you are just getting started, you will need to create some type of budget that will enable you to start building the reserves you will need to invest in real estate. If you don't have 3-6 months of reserves saved, that needs to be your first goal.

When I was in my early 20's, my ability to "budget" was much more difficult. However, if you want to become a Boss Lady Investor, and especially if you want to become a Boss Lady Real Estate Investor, you have to find creative (and sometimes painful) ways to save.

Years ago, when my paychecks and lifestyle were a lot leaner, it looked more like this:

- 95% to checking account to cover bills.
- 5% to savings, CD or mutual funds, or I would make an extra mortgage payment on my primary residence.

As my income increased, I used the extra money to pay more toward my debts. As I paid off one debt, I rolled to the next one and became obsessed with paying off debts.

A credit score that won't make a lender flinch. If your credit is in the toilet, don't flush your dreams just yet. I scraped my way back from a score in the low 500s. It takes time, commitment and a plan, but I have helped many beginner Boss Ladies fix their credit to go on to become Boss Ladies extraordinaire.

If you're nodding along and have all four of these areas covered—high five! Boss Lady, you are ready to rock and roll in real estate investing. If not, pause here. Go read my first book or talk to a financial coach. Because without a solid base, real estate can quickly become a money pit instead of a wealth builder.

Be Ready for
♫ The Man ♫

Nothing kills momentum faster than falling for a house you can't afford. Before you start shopping for real:

- Pull your credit report. Fix any errors.
- Gather tax returns, pay stubs, and bank statements.
- Shop lenders. Get quotes from a few.
- Get a pre-approval letter.

Your lender will let you know what the bank says you can afford so you aren't losing time making offers on homes that are out of your range. This also lets sellers know you're serious and helps you move fast when you find "the one".

And if you're serious about becoming a real estate investor, you need to come to the table ready to rock and roll. This means being reliable, prepared, organized, and respectful of the time and energy of the people helping you: your real estate agent, lender, contractor, and/or business partner. If you're constantly flaking on calls, unsure of your budget, or dragging your feet on paperwork, they'll stop prioritizing you and eventually, they'll stop working with you altogether. In this business, time is money, and no one wants to waste theirs.

So, what does coming to the table prepared look like? It means having your financial ducks in a row: your credit score pulled, pre-approval letter in hand, proof of funds available, budget range established, and a basic understanding of the market you're buying in. It's okay to be new, but it's not okay to be sloppy. The more dialed in you are, the faster your team can help you succeed and the more respected you'll be as a Boss Lady Investor.

Build Your Dream Team
♫ *You Belong with Me* ♫

You do not have to do this alone. A solid crew is your secret weapon. Your core dream team needs to include:

- A rockstar real estate agent (investor-friendly). This isn't just me (I am a licensed realtor), but also a team of other real estate agents ready to find deals and strike when they are hot.
- A lender who explains things clearly.
- An inspector who finds EVERYTHING.
- Contractors (roofer, electrician, plumber, carpenter, handyman, pest control provider) who show up and don't ghost.
- A CPA who knows real estate deductions.
- A mentor or investing buddy to sanity-check deals.

Interview people. Ask for referrals. Trust your gut. If they talk down to you or rush you, bye.

> **ROCKSTAR TIP**
>
> Build relationships with your contractors.Treat them well. They will save you thousands.

One of the most powerful tools in your investing journey isn't money, it's your network. Building strong relationships will open more doors than any spreadsheet ever could. Make your presence known: attend Chamber of Commerce events, support fundraisers and causes that matter to your team, and be visible in your community. Give back not because it looks good, but because it feels good, and people notice.

Your reputation is just as critical to your financial future as your credit score. People want to do business with those they like, trust, and see acting consistently. Send a handwritten thank-you note to your lender after closing. Invite your insurance agent to play in a charity pickleball tournament, or better yet, find out what causes they care about and show up to their events. That's how real relationships are built.

The most successful investors I know, they're involved. They engage. They understand that meaningful relationships lead to meaningful opportunities. When you show the community you care, it will show up for you in return with referrals, partnerships, and trust you simply can't buy.

Keep Your Eye on The End Game

Say it one more time: *Done is better than perfect.*

You will never know everything. You will make mistakes. Taking imperfect action beats waiting for the stars to align.

Start with one deal. Learn. Adjust. Scale up.

And after you buy that first property (because the journey doesn't stop with the keys in your hand), it's just the beginning. There is still plenty more work ahead. We will also go over the post-purchase essentials:

- Identifying cash-on-cash opportunities (your true return on investment!). For me, this might be add-ons in a vacation rental, like early check-in fees or pet fees.
- Managing mortgages and debt. Don't lose your money to late fees or extra charges. Pay your bills on time, every time, and build your credit into a powerhouse tool.
- Pulling equity from existing investments. Use leverage to scale your portfolio (more on that later).
- Building systems so you don't lose your sanity.
- Creating smart partnerships (and avoiding bad ones).
- Scaling from one-to-many properties (without drowning in the details).
- What to expect as a landlord—property management companies, repairs and updating your investments. Real estate investing can become a "set it and forget it", but it's not that at all in the beginning. Be prepared to work for it.

Real estate is powerful. But it's not magic. It takes vision, patience, and action. Spoiler alert: Real estate is NOT a "get-rich-quick" game. I may have gotten lucky with a big sale in Florida (hello, Hawaii vacation!), but trust me, years of research, learning, and building my portfolio set me up for success. That "luck"? It was a combo of planning and opportunity. You can create your version of that "luck," too.

Celebrate Wins and Keep Growing
Get ♫ Down Bad ♫

Real estate investing is a journey. Celebrate every milestone:

- First deal? Pop champagne.
- First rent check? Dinner out.
- Paid off a mortgage? Plan a trip.

Stay humble, stay hungry, stay kind. Teach other women. We rise together.

Once you learn how to do this, I hope you'll take your knowledge and use it to help others. Sharing knowledge isn't just about giving back; it is about lifting as we climb. But let me be clear: helping others doesn't mean giving your knowledge away for free.

While I'm all for mentorship and meaningful conversations, an hour of your time, experience, and hard-earned wisdom is worth more than a five-dollar latte. I've had people ask me for free copies of this very book, the one that took me months to write, decades to live, and everything I had to create. If someone isn't willing to spend fifteen bucks and a few hours learning? Boss Lady moment of truth: they probably aren't serious about applying your advice anyway.

You can still help others by pointing them in the right direction—recommend websites, podcasts, resources, and yes, this book. But they need to have skin in the game. Support and generosity are powerful, but there's a big difference between helping someone grow and letting yourself be taken advantage of.

Know your worth. Protect your energy. And when you give, give from a place of strength, not sacrifice.

You now have a roadmap:

ROCKSTAR ROADMAP

Pick a lane.
Learn the basics.
Build your team.
Fund your dream.
Take action.
Repeat.

By the end of this book, you'll know exactly how to find, buy, fund, manage, and profit from your first real estate investment. No fluff. Just real talk, real tools, and real wealth.

Grab your pen, check your credit, and pour another coffee, you're officially on the path to becoming the Boss Lady Investor you were always meant to be.

This is your era.

Chapter 3
LONG-TERM RENTALS

The OG Real Estate Investment
♬ *Like a Virgin* ♬

Alright, dream-chasing Boss Ladies, roll up those sleeves, pour yourself a strong cup of coffee (we'll pop that celebratory bubbly *after* you close your first deal), and let's dig into what might be the single most important, steady move you make to build real, reliable, repeatable wealth: buying your first long-term rental property.

This is where it all begins.

Think of buying your first long-term rental like, well ... *your first time*. It might not be perfect, it might feel a little awkward, and you might second-guess yourself a dozen times, but once you've done it, a whole new world opens. You start to understand the power you hold. You gain confidence. You stop just thinking about financial freedom and start living it.

Long-term rentals are the OG of real estate investing, the *"Like a Virgin"* of wealth-building. It's classic, it's foundational, and it still hits all the right notes. While they might not be as flashy as flips or as Instagrammable as vacation rentals, they're stable, predictable, and incredibly effective at helping you build real wealth over time. They are also typically a little easier to get funding for than vacation rentals or flips.

Long-term residential rentals can be the ideal starting point because you're not reinventing the wheel. You're simply learning how to analyze numbers, work with tenants, understand cash flow, and grow equity all in a relatively controlled environment. And once you get one under your belt, the next one comes more easily, and the one after that even more so.

I know. It's not shimmery. And regardless how "traditional" long-term rentals may be as an investor starting point, they are still a little intimidating, too.

When it comes to real estate, there are as many strategies as there are brands of designer purses. You might be tempted by shiny trends: quick flips, swanky short-term Airbnb's, buying tax liens, wholesaling foreclosures, but guess what? Every seasoned investor I know has a classic, boring-but-beautiful bread-and-butter piece holding up their empire: a good old long-term rental.

Think of it like your timeless, black Coach bag: dependable, practical, and it *always* shows up for you. This is your staple piece. It won't make you famous on TikTok, but it will pay your bills, build your equity, and give you the kind of financial calm that lets you sleep easy at night.

If you're ready for passive income, growing net worth, and freedom to pick up and adventure on your terms, buckle up.

I'm about to give you the step-by-step blueprint I used to build my own long-term rental empire, from my first single-family fixer to a portfolio that pays me while I sip mojitos on the beach.

Backstory: My First, Accidental Long-Term Rental

♫ *Live to Tell* ♫

Picture this: I was dating this great guy (now my husband), who owned a townhouse. Meanwhile, I was staring down the barrel of foreclosure after a crumbled marriage and a real estate market that went from boom to bust overnight. The obvious move was for my daughter and I to pack it up and move into his place, right?

Wrong. Negative, Bat-Lady. *Obvious* isn't always *optimal.*

See, my daughter Kiki had been through more *trauma* in her short nine years than most adults. Adoption. Divorce. Bio mom, bio dad, and my now-ex-husband-who-she-had-called-"dad" all vanished from her life without a trace. Stability was everything. Uprooting her from our community, her school, and her people? Not an option. We made the decision to keep Kiki grounded, to stay in the school system and community where she was comfortable. This would mean we would need to rent out his townhouse.

Hello, Landlady Life.

Selling the townhouse would have been optimal, but this was mid-Great Recession. The value had tanked since my then boyfriend (now hubby) first purchased the townhouse. The mortgage balance owed was around $150,000, and the market was only offering $100,000 if we sold. So, we pivoted, rented it out, and became landlords by default. And that, my friend, was my first taste of passive income, though it certainly didn't feel passive at all.

Now, there is a little more to the story. I'll cover that when I talk about House Hacking later in this chapter.

Back to our story. Kiki and I lived in the house that I had purchased with my ex. The one that was about to be foreclosed on as part of my pending bankruptcy. How did I get to that point? Honestly, by biting off more than I could chew in the middle of a crumbling relationship. All in all, I made a really bad decision and would end up paying for it for years.

We paid $408,000 when "we" bought it. During the Recession, the house plummeted to a market value of $240,000. We divorced. When my ex left, he did not pay a cent towards the house, nor child support of any kind (unless you count the $45 he sent me for three months for my daughter's dance lessons until even that stopped). I did the math. Even if my daughter and I stayed in the house and paid for ten years, there would be no gain and no equity. Foreclosing was my best option. It was wildly painful, yet I did it with dignity. We left the home clean, communicated throughout the process with the bank, and even received a payment from the mortgage lender through a deal called "Cash For Keys" (a popular program during the Great Recession). Bonus: it would have been weird for me to start my new life while staying in a house mired in bad memories, so there was a silver lining.

Fast forward: My then boyfriend and now (final) husband found a new house in Kiki's school zone which happened to *also* be a foreclosure (foreclosures were extremely common during this time). We gave a low offer and got the house for a steal. We managed to keep her in the same neighborhood, same school, same village. Over time, we built equity in the house while collecting rent on the townhouse. When we sold the townhouse ten years later, we pocketed over $50,000! We took the win, rolled it into new investments, and continued our march toward financial freedom.

My credit was decimated after the foreclosure and bankruptcy. So how did I buy a house with that on my credit? I hate admitting this part almost as much as I love how blessed I was that it happened. Colin, my now husband, put the loan in his name only (since there was no way I would qualify). The deed, however, was in *both* of our names. Why? Because we would *both* be contributing to the home even if my credit was a mess.

I have seen so many Boss Ladies get screwed by not demanding they go on a deed. If you are cohabitating and contributing to the home, get your name on that deed sister. Write out an agreement, *in advance*, of what the home equity will look like *should things not work out.*

If your partner won't agree to put you on a deed on a home you share, *they are not the right partner.*

I hope you don't end up in a situation like I did, but if you find yourself forced into a tough decision—foreclosure, a breakup, job loss—just know real estate can still be your way forward. Some of the best investments come from the messiest moments. You must be willing to see the opportunity inside the chaos.

Moral of the story? Your first deal doesn't have to be perfect. It just needs to get you started.

While my first rental property was accidental, the next one was not. The next investment was strategic. It was an investment made with intention.

Choosing a Property

Location, Location, Location
The ♫ Borderline ♫

Let's decode this cliché into something real. Many newbies blow this step. They buy the cheap house with zero demand, or they overpay in a "hot" market that turns cold the second interest rates rise or companies relocate.

Here's my simple rule: skip the hype, buy the *predictable*. You want a "Steady Eddie" neighborhood. These areas have:

- Stable, middle-class residents.
- Good schools. Families stick around.
- Nearby jobs and steady employers: think hospitals, military bases, colleges.
- Grocery stores, parks, and decent coffee shops.
- Low crime rates.
- Areas that aren't the highest end or the lowest end, the ones on the borderline.

Talk to locals. I once confirmed my gut on a deal because the barista told me, "Oh, that street is full of nurses and teachers, no trouble there." Real estate pros call it "boots on the ground intel". I call it coffee gossip. Either way, it works.

> **ROCKSTAR TIP**
> To get a good feeling for the neighborhood, drive by on different days and at different times.

Identify the general area where you want to buy your first investment, your borderlines. Then start watching Zillow like it's your first dating profile. Check out new listings when they show up. Follow price trends, identify what "ballpark" you will be playing in.

Pick a
♬ Lucky Star ♬

Ladies, remember when you are looking at properties that this is an investment. This is not your dream home. It's a reliable rental. That means you need to think like a landlord, not a Pinterest addict. An ideal starter rental looks like this:

2-3 bedrooms, 1-2 baths. The sweet spot for young couples, retirees or small families.

No weird layouts. People want bedrooms with doors, not a random attic loft advertised as a "third bedroom." If you like weird layouts, there is a place for that in Chapter 4. But don't start there.

Low maintenance yard. Tenants don't want to mow an acre. Neither do you.

Solid bones. Older is fine, just make sure the foundation and other major items are solid or in a renovation budget.

Deals. Buying and then renovating your first rental may be too much for some, but if it's up your alley (and fits your budget), then finding a property that needs a little TLC prior to rental and can be purchased for a steal may yield an awesome payout.

I have a simple test: *If my college-aged self would have lived here and felt safe, it's probably good enough for tenants.*

Your Must-Know Glossary

Here's where the amateurs separate from the Boss Ladies.

Boss Ladies come to the table prepared. We have done our research and crunched the numbers.

Cash Flow. Money left after all expenses (mortgage, taxes, insurance, repairs).

Cap Rate. Annual income divided by purchase price. Good for comparing deals.

ARV (After Repair Value). What a property will be worth after you fix it up.

Revenue. The total money your property or business brings in before any expenses are taken out. Think of it as all the cash coming *in the door* aka your top-line earnings.

Gross Revenue. The *total* income generated from your property including rent, cleaning fees, pet fees, and any extras (like parking or laundry) before subtracting *any* expenses.

BACKSTAGE PASS

Be careful! People often use these terms inconsistently.

Net Revenue. What's left after you've paid for all operating expenses (like management, maintenance, utilities, and cleaning). This is often called your Net Operating Income (NOI) and shows how much your property actually *earns you* before taxes or mortgage payments.

Income. Your overall money *earned* from all sources, not just rentals. This can include salary, side hustles, investments, and rental revenue. It's the cash flow that fuels your freedom.

Rental Income. Money you earn from tenants or guests paying to stay in your property. This can be monthly rent for long-term rentals or nightly rates for vacation rentals.

Example: If your beach house rents for $350 a night for 20 nights, your rental income is $7,000 that month.

> **ROCKSTAR TIP**
> Track expenses religiously. The IRS rewards organized investors with great write-offs.

Expenses. Everything you spend to own, operate, and maintain your property—cleaning, repairs, marketing, management fees, supplies, and more.

> **ROCKSTAR TIP**
> Always keep at least three to six months of expenses in reserves.

Reserves. Money you set aside each month as a safety net for unexpected costs like clogged plumbing, A/C repair, or mold remediation. Always keep at least 3 to 6 months of expenses in reserves.

CapEx Fund (Capital Expenditures Fund). A special savings bucket for *big* property improvements like replacing a roof, remodeling a kitchen, or buying new furniture for your Airbnb. These aren't everyday expenses, they're the "big-ticket" updates that protect your investment's value.

Equity. The portion of your property you *own outright.* It's the difference between your property's current market value and what you still owe on the mortgage.

Example: If your home is worth $500,000 and you owe $350,000, you have $150,000 in equity.

Leverage. Using other people's money (usually through loans) to buy or grow your real estate portfolio. Smart leverage lets you own more properties and grow faster without needing all the cash up-front.

Cash-on-Cash Return (CoC or Cash-on-Cash Investing). This tells you how much *cash flow* you earn compared to the *actual cash* you invested in a property. It tells you the annual return on the money you've personally put in, not including appreciation or mortgage paydown, just your out-of-pocket investment versus your yearly profit.

> **ROCKSTAR TIP**
> Use CoC Return to compare deals and evaluate your property's performance.

CASH-ON-CASH RETURN (%) =
ANNUAL CASH FLOW ÷ TOTAL CASH INVESTED

Example: If you invest $50,000 into a rental property and earn $6,000 a year in cash flow after expenses, your cash-on-cash return is 12% ($6,000 ÷ $50,000).

Monthly Carrying Cost. The total amount it costs you each month to *carry* the property, including mortgage, taxes, insurance, HOA fees, and utilities. This is also called "holding cost". Think of this as your monthly "stay afloat" number. *You must be confident in the monthly carrying cost before making an offer.* Let's do a deeper dive on what is included here.

Mortgage payment. How much will it be? You should have already done your research on lenders and rates; now choose the best one and nail down the mortgage payments. Don't forget to include mortgage insurance if your lender requires it.

Property taxes. This number needs to be based on the purchase price YOU pay. Often when people buy property, they look at the property taxes the current owner pays and think that is what they will pay. Not so. Your taxes will be based on the purchase price YOU pay. If you purchase the home for $300,000 and the former owner purchased it for $120,000 twenty years ago, you are going to have much higher taxes than the current owner is paying. On top of that, you are purchasing as an investor, meaning, you won't qualify for any homestead exemptions on the property.

Insurance. Get quotes, get quotes, get quotes. Don't assume one quote is the standard as rates can be all over the place. We just got two quotes on the same property, one for $4,500 and the other $8,000. Get quotes.

HOA fees (if any, I avoid them!). If you are buying a condo, make sure you check on any pending assessments. The last thing you want is to buy a condo then three months later be hit with a massive assessment. Also, double check the rental rules with the condo association. You need to know the rules on the property you buy. Find out how often the HOA fees have gone up in the past.

Repairs & maintenance. Budget at least 1% of the home value annually for repairs and maintenance. If you are renovating, you can use a lower number for the first few years.

Property management fees (if you hire help).

Add it all up. This is your monthly carrying cost.

A Backstage Pass
♫ *Secret* ♫

In the world of real estate investing, people often toss around terms like they mean the same thing, even when they don't. Take *monthly carrying costs* and *expenses*, for example. Or *revenue*, *gross revenue*, and *net revenue*—all of which get casually lumped together as just "revenue." The key is to make sure you know **exactly which numbers** are being discussed.

I've seen many investors get tripped up thinking a property's *net* revenue was X when they were actually looking at *gross* revenue, or assume expenses meant *all costs* when it really only covered monthly carrying costs. Always clarify the numbers before you crunch them.

Understanding Cash Flow

Now that you know the monthly carrying cost, you can estimate the rent and calculate the cash flow.

Run the Numbers
♫ *Justify My Love* ♫

First, you need to estimate the rent. How do you do this? Use Zillow, social media, or better yet ask a local property manager. Be conservative. The "Zestimate" on Zillow does not guarantee that's what the owner will end up getting.

Try to find out what the actual rents nearby are, then stay a little under the market for your estimate. It's better to be safe than sorry on this one. You don't want to overestimate only to find out you aren't making enough in rent to cover your bills. That's the *opposite* of investing, that's just losing money.

BASIC RULE

Revenue - Expenses = Cash Flow

If the positive cash flow is only fifty bucks a month? Keep looking. You are going to want a buffer for vacancies and surprise repairs such as that time the water heater explodes at 2:00 am (ask me how I know). Consider questions like:

- What if you have a 2-month vacancy?
- What if property taxes jump? In Florida, we had a 60% increase in insurance and 20-50% increases in taxes in one year alone.
- What if a big employer leaves town?
- What if there is a big HOA assessment?

ROCKSTAR TIP

Stress test your cash flow. Run the numbers repeatedly to reflect the impact of risks.

Plan for the worst and be pleasantly surprised when the normal months roll in with extra cash.

Cash Flow Investing

I personally invest primarily for cash flow. That means I focus on properties that generate consistent monthly income after all expenses are paid. This type of investing is about creating steady, predictable revenue, the kind that pays the bills, builds financial freedom, and gives you options. But here's the beautiful bonus: while I invest for cash flow, real estate *tends* to appreciate over time. That means my properties often go up in value, and when they do, I benefit from capital appreciation all while someone else (my tenant or guest) is paying down the mortgage.

Cash flow investing is different from other strategies like speculative appreciation investing, where the goal is to buy low and sell high, often without strong monthly income in the meantime. Some investors buy in hot markets and bank on future value increases, and while that can work, it's riskier and more dependent on timing. There's also fix-and-flip investing, which is focused on short-term gains and quick turnarounds rather than long-term income. I do some of that too, when it makes sense, but most of my wealth building is done with longer term cash-on-cash investing.

The way I see it? Cash flow creates stability and options now, while appreciation builds wealth over time. You don't have to choose just one style of investing, but you should understand which strategy aligns best with your goals, risk tolerance, and lifestyle. For me, there's nothing more powerful than an asset that pays you monthly, appreciates in value, and lets someone else fund your future in the process. That's the kind of investing I can get behind.

The 1% Rule

Let's take a minute to talk about one of the most well-known real estate investing benchmarks—the 1% Rule. For years, investors (including me) used this rule of thumb to quickly evaluate potential deals: if the monthly rent equals at least 1% of the purchase price, it's likely a solid cash-flowing property.

For example, a $200,000 property should ideally bring in at least $2,000/month in rent.

> **THE 1% RULE**
> A rental income at least 1% of the purchase price will likely have positive cash flow.

But here's the truth in today's market: that benchmark is getting harder to hit. With housing prices rising faster than rents in many areas, the 1% Rule has become more of a unicorn than a norm in some markets.

Many investors today are seeing returns closer to 0.6%–0.8% of the purchase price in monthly rent. That means a $300,000 home may only bring in $1,800 to $2,400/month, and that squeeze can make a big difference in your bottom line. Lower margins leave less room for error, surprise expenses, or periods of vacancy.

That's why you've got to be even more diligent. Run your numbers. Double-check your math. Stress-test your projected cash flow. And if the deal doesn't provide a positive cash flow? Walk away. It doesn't matter how cute the house is or how much "potential" it has, if it's not putting money in your pocket each month, it's a liability, not an asset.

Markets ebb and flow. There are times, and places, where 1.5% or even 2% returns are possible. But don't count on it. Use conservative estimates, stay realistic, and always prioritize positive cash flow. That's how you stay in the game long enough to win it.

Get ♫ Into the Groove ♫

Every investment boils down to this: *Do the numbers make sense?* Always, always, always run the numbers before you fall in love with a cute porch.

Here is a very basic example:

EXAMPLE 1	
INVESTMENT	
Purchase price	200,000
MONTHLY EXPENSES	
Mortgage, taxes, insurance	(1,400)
MONTHLY REVENUE	2,000
MONTHLY CASH FLOW	600

Winner!

Now, run the numbers again, this time setting aside reserves for maintenance and vacancy (5-10%). Be conservative. Hope for the best, plan for the worst.

EXAMPLE 1, WITH RESERVES	
INVESTMENT	
Purchase price	200,000
MONTHLY EXPENSES	
Mortgage, taxes, insurance	(1,400)
Reserves, 10%	(140)
MONTHLY REVENUE	2,000
MONTHLY CASH FLOW	460

Still a winner!

Hiccups are Normal

Let's talk about something that rarely gets mentioned but absolutely should.

You're probably going to have to reinvest in your investment before you ever see real profits.

There's a high likelihood that something will go wrong in the first few years that costs you money, and it might feel like a punch to the gut. Maybe it's a roof leak, a busted hot water heater, a broken A/C, or a refrigerator that decides to quit during peak season. And here's the kicker: you might not have made enough money yet to cover these expenses.

That's normal. And it's okay.

This is part of the process. It doesn't mean you made a bad decision or that you're failing; it just means you're in the early stages of owning a real, income-producing asset. The beginning is often the messiest and most uncertain part of the journey.

Yes, it's frustrating when it feels like the money is going out faster than it's coming in. But seasoned investors will tell you —this is how it starts. You're not doing anything wrong. You're learning, growing, and building something that will serve you in the long run.

The key is to plan for the hiccups, emotionally and financially. Set aside reserves. Expect the unexpected. Because once you accept that real estate investing is a long game, the short-term setbacks won't shake you.

Over time, you'll get used to these surprise expenses and start seeing them as just another part of doing business. But in the beginning? Give yourself grace. You're not just buying property; you're building wealth, one learning curve at a time.

Fund Like a
 ♫ *Material Girl* ♫

Owning one rental house is nice. But multiple houses using smart leverage? That's how you build an empire.

However, new investors are often stumped with how to buy more than one home. They remember how hard it was just to get the mortgage on the home they live in. But don't worry, Boss Lady, there are plenty of ways you can pay for a long-term rental investment.

The more common routes are:

Conventional mortgage. With these loans, you will want to plan to put 20–30% as a down payment. While your primary residence may have required much less down (likely 3.5-20%), when you are buying an investment property the down payment is higher. That's because lenders realize you are more likely to default on a property you don't happen to live in than one you do (also, in some states, primary residences are protected from debt collectors, whereas investment properties are not). This type of loan will typically have the lowest interest rate of all your options. The purchased property will be collateral and if you default on your payments, you lose the house.

HELOC (Home Equity Line of Credit). Tap equity from your primary home. Let's say your house is worth $400,000 but you only owe $200,000. You may be able to use the "equity", or the difference between what the house is worth and what you owe, to obtain a loan to purchase a rental property (in this case $400,000 - $200,000 = $200,000). Keep in mind, no bank will give you the "full equity" (nor should they, as the Great Recession proved), but they will often lend up to 70 or 80% of your home value. $200,000 x 70% = $140,000 HELOC). Keep in mind, your primary residence is the collateral for this type of loan.

Side note: There is a difference between a Home Equity Line of Credit (HELOC) and a Commercial Line of Credit (LOC). A HELOC is typically tied to your primary residence (the "home" in HELOC). A commercial line-of-credit operates almost identically (albeit with a higher interest rate) but is tied to an investment property.

Owner-occupied Loan. This is traditionally known as house hacking. Buy a home, rent out rooms to your friends (or strangers) to cover the mortgage. Be careful here as these loans have specifications (for example, you must live in the home yourself). I've seen beginner investors use VA and FHA loans to get started. We'll talk more about the various types of loans later in the book. Another note of caution: know your local codes about how many people can live in an owner-occupied home as many cities have a one-family rule and other regulations.

Partnership. Team up with a trusted friend or family member. Share the costs and profits. These work great if everyone works well together, but steer clear of partners that you will likely clash with or that have different end games. It's no fun to think you are buying a house to hold onto for twenty years only to find out your partner in the property wants to cash out after five. Have the hard talks *before* you buy property together.

Hard Money. Hard money refers to short-term real estate loans funded by private investors or specialized lenders rather than traditional banks. These loans are typically based more on the value of the property (the "hard asset") than on the borrower's credit score or income. These loans are not typically ideal for long-term rentals, but useful if you buy a fixer and refi. I've used hard money to buy fixer-uppers then, after the rehabilitation, decided to keep them as rentals, so I then paid off the hard money loan with a conventional loan.

Commercial Loan. Once you're established, you will be able to start using commercial loans and even commercial LOC's (lines of credit). A commercial loan in real estate is a mortgage used to finance income-producing properties that are typically owned for business or investment purposes rather than personal use. These include apartment complexes, vacation rentals, office buildings, retail centers, warehouses, hotels, and mixed-use properties—basically, anything that generates revenue. Unlike residential loans (which are based mostly on your personal income and credit), commercial loans are usually underwritten based on the property's income potential, measured through metrics like Net Operating Income (NOI) and Debt Service Coverage Ratio (DSCR).

We will review these options in more detail in Chapters 7 and 8.

Shop around. Compare interest rates. And always read the fine print. I once caught a sneaky balloon payment buried in a loan doc—would have cost me $20,000 at renewal. Know how to read a mortgage loan statement and review the documents before signing them. There is nothing worse than a Boss Lady building her dreams only to find out it's going to take longer than she thought because she didn't do her research and homework. Make sure you understand what you are signing *before* you sign it.

It's important to know to read your closing documents (when you buy the house) and your mortgage statement (once the house is yours).

How to Read Your Closing Documents

Closing day can feel like signing your life away, but understanding the big pieces will keep you in control.

Here's what matters most:

Loan Estimate (LE). You'll get this early in the process. It outlines your loan amount, interest rate, estimated payments, and closing costs. Think of it as your preview.

Closing Disclosure (CD). The final version of your Loan Estimate. Double-check every number here—especially your interest rate, loan amount, cash to close, and monthly payment—to ensure nothing changed unexpectedly.

Promissory Note. Your written promise to repay the loan. It details your rate, term, and payment schedule.

Deed of Trust or Mortgage. This gives the lender a legal claim to the property if you stop making payments.

Title Documents. Show that the property legally transfers to you, free of liens or ownership issues.

Escrow & Tax Disclosures. Outline what funds are being held for taxes and insurance.

Settlement Statement (ALTA or HUD-1). The master list of where every penny goes: your down payment, seller credits, fees, and loan funds. Look this over closely. While most of the time the title company or attorney will get this right, I have had multiple closings where I found money that needed to be credited to me on the HUD-1 that ended up with adjustments being made in my favor.

How to Read Your Mortgage Statement

Your monthly mortgage statement may look intimidating, but it's really just a snapshot of what you owe and where your money is going. Here's what to look for:

Principal. This is the amount going toward paying down your loan balance each month. (This is what builds your equity!)

Interest. The cost of borrowing the money. Early on, this is the biggest part of your payment.

Escrow. Funds held for property taxes and insurance. Your lender pays these on your behalf.

Fees or PMI/MIP. Private Mortgage Insurance (PMI) or Mortgage Insurance Premium (MIP) if required. These usually drop off once you've built enough equity.

Loan Balance. What you still owe on the mortgage. Watch this go down every month—it's financial progress in action.

Year-to-Date Totals. Track how much of your payments have gone to principal versus interest. (A great reminder to make an extra payment or two toward principal when you can!)

If your goal is to pay your home off faster, look for the "Principal" number in the "Payment Breakdown" section on your statement. Add even small amounts to this number each month—it makes a huge difference over time.

ROCKSTAR TIP

Pay extra on your mortgage. You'll reduce the total interest paid and pay off the loan faster.

From Wreck to Rent Check

♫ *Like a Prayer* ♫

That leads me to my next topic: inspections. Get an inspection done on the property. If you are getting a great "deal" on the purchase price, there are likely reasons. Reasons that could be extremely expensive like a new roof could be needed or the wiring in the house could be outdated. Find a good inspector and get the inspection done so that you know exactly what you are getting into. Plus, inspectors often find issues that may give you an opportunity to ask the seller to give you credits, concessions or even have the seller repair the issue.

Don't forget to also reach out to insurance agents during this time to make sure the house is insurable and that the cost of insurance fits into your budget.

Let me tell you something, Boss Lady, what looks like a disaster to most people is often a hidden goldmine to an investor with vision. That peeling paint, broken windows, and jungle of a yard? That's opportunity in disguise.

When I bought my first "fixer-upper," it was the kind of place that made people raise their eyebrows and mutter, *"Are you sure?"* But I didn't see the holes in the drywall; I saw cash flow. I didn't see the dated linoleum; I saw a modern rental that could bring in steady income month after month.

The rehab process wasn't glamorous. There were unexpected plumbing issues, a surprise electrical panel that needed upgrading, and a learning curve that could humble anyone. But I leaned into the chaos, built a team of trusted contractors, kept a tight budget, and tackled one project at a time. Flooring, paint, fixtures, appliances, all upgraded with renters in mind. Durable, affordable, and stylish.

Four months later, what was once a neighborhood eyesore became the most in-demand rental on the block. The transformation added tens of thousands in equity. And the monthly rent checks? Chef's kiss. That property became a cornerstone in my portfolio. I still own it today.

The moral of the story? Don't fear the ugly ducklings. With strategy, sweat equity, and a little courage, you can turn rundown into revenue and build wealth one rehab at a time.

Landlady Life

Screening
♫ *Beautiful Strangers* ♫

Once your rental property is ready to rent, it's time to get a tenant!

A bad tenant can wreck your cash flow and your sanity so make sure you have a plan in place on how you screen your tenants. Here are my golden rules for screening:

Minimum income 3x rent. If rent is $2,000/month, then your tenant needs a household income of at least $6,000/month.

Verify employment. Call HR if needed. An unemployed tenant is often a non-paying tenant.

Run a credit check. Look for a history of paying bills. I don't look for perfect credit on many of my units, but I do look for glaring signs that the person does or does not act responsibly.

New landladies can easily run a credit check on potential tenants using trusted screening services like TransUnion SmartMove, Experian Connect, or RentPrep—all of which handle the tenant's authorization securely. Always get written consent before running a report, review key factors like payment history and debt levels, and follow Fair Housing and Fair Credit laws if you deny an applicant based on their credit. A clear, consistent screening process protects both your property and your peace of mind.

Run a background check. Landladies can run background checks through the same trusted tenant-screening services they use for credit reports. Always get written consent from the applicant, review results for criminal or eviction history, and make sure to follow Fair Housing and privacy laws when making rental decisions. This step also helps ensure your property—and your peace of mind—are well protected.

Call past landlords. The real story comes out fast.

Interview. Meet them (or have your property manager meet them). Trust your gut.

Listen, I can't mislead you—I have not stuck to these rules with every tenant. Markets change and sometimes you must adjust and pivot. Know that when you "overlook" requirements however, you are putting yourself at risk for future issues. Just make sure to understand the risk you are taking before you take it.

Lease Agreements *♫ Express Yourself ♫ Clearly*

There's plenty of debate about lease length in the rental world. Some landlords swear you should always have a signed long-term lease, collect the security deposit, and receive the first month's rent before handing over the keys, and I agree with that in most cases. A long-term lease (typically 6–12 months) gives you stability, predictable income, and legal protection if issues come up.

That said, a month-to-month lease is still a signed, legally binding agreement, just with more flexibility. It automatically renews each month until either party gives proper notice (usually 30 days). This can be incredibly useful in certain markets or with tenants you don't know well yet because it's easier to end the tenancy if problems arise. The downside? It's also easier for the tenant to leave unexpectedly, which can mean vacancies.

In both cases, you should always collect a security deposit to cover potential damages. The main difference is that with a month-to-month lease, you only collect one month's rent at a time, while a long-term lease often allows you to collect additional rent up-front or enforce stricter penalties for breaking the lease early.

Boss Lady Takeaway: Both lease types have their place—long-term for stability, month-to-month for flexibility. Choose the one that keeps your cash flow (and your stress level) steady. This business is about building wealth—but never at the expense of your health or peace of mind.

A solid lease agreement is your first line of protection as a landlord. It sets expectations, prevents misunderstandings, and gives you legal backing if issues arise. Whether you're renting a room, a long-term home, or a vacation property, these are the non-negotiables every lease should cover:

Critical elements of the lease:

Names of All Parties. Include every tenant (and co-signer) who will live there.

Property Details. Exact address and a clear description of what's included (garage, yard, appliances, etc.).

Lease Term. Start and end dates, renewal terms, and what happens if the tenant stays past the lease period.

Rent Amount & Due Date. Spell out how much, when it's due, accepted payment methods, and late-fee policies.

Security Deposit Details. How much, where it's held (if required by state law), and what conditions determine its return.

Utilities & Maintenance. Who pays for what (electricity, lawn care, pest control, etc.) and who handles repairs.

Occupancy Rules. Who can live there and what happens if guests stay long-term.

Pet Policy. Clear rules, fees, or restrictions if you allow pets.

Use of Property & Restrictions. No illegal activities, subletting, or unauthorized modifications.

Entry & Inspection Rights. The notice you must give before entering, as required by state law.

Default & Eviction Terms. What happens if rent isn't paid or the lease is broken.

Signatures & Date. Every adult tenant and the landlord must sign; verbal agreements don't hold up in court.

Boss Ladies don't need to reinvent the wheel—there are reliable, state-specific lease templates available from:

State Realtor Associations (often the most legally thorough)

Online platforms like Avial.com, LawDepot, Rocket Lawyer, or BiggerPockets

Local property management companies or landlord associations (great for regional compliance)

Your real estate attorney, especially for multi-unit or short-term rentals

Always review your lease with an attorney or experienced property manager the first time you rent a property. One solid, legally tight lease can save you thousands, and many headaches, down the road.

ROCKSTAR TIP

Review your lease agreement with an attorney the first time you rent a property.

Repairs & Upkeep

♫ *Keep it Together* ♫

Big girls don't cry in real estate, but you will find yourself curled up on the couch sobbing if you don't save for repairs.

Create a maintenance fund. Set aside 1–2% of property value per year for normal repairs. This is what is "generally suggested." You will need to figure out what amount works for you.

Create a CapEx Fund. A CapEx (Capital Expenditure) fund is your savings account for the big stuff-roofs, HVAC systems, water heaters, and major appliances. These aren't "if" expenses; they're when expenses. For the first few years I own a property, I put any extra income directly into my CapEx fund until it's fully stocked. That way, when something big breaks (and it will), I'm not scrambling or dipping into personal savings. A well-prepared Boss Lady knows those big-ticket repairs are coming—and she's ready for them.

Fix little things fast. A tiny leak becomes a mold nightmare in weeks. Plus, nothing irritates good tenants faster than feeling ignored. If you show your tenants that *you* care about the property, they are more likely to care about the property back.

Another key detail—make sure the property is rent ready *before* you start renting it. That makes it possible to create that CapEx fund because you will buy yourself years before a major repair happens. For example, if you spend all your money on a house that has a twenty-five year old roof you may find yourself in deep water when a huge storm comes through and suddenly you need another $10,000 or more; whereas, a newer roof before you start renting will give you many years of building up the coffers before you have to reach in. Your rental needs to be ready to go before the first renter moves in.

> **ROCKSTAR TIP**
> Put repairs on a card that earns rewards ONLY IF you pay the balance in full every month.

Here's a Boss Lady strategy that is great for some but can become catastrophic for others so *know thyself.* If you are great with credit cards (and if you are not, run from this sister), put your repairs and maintenance on a card that gets you rewards for travel, cash back, Amazon, whatever makes you happy. Pay them off every month from the bank account that you have hopefully set up for the property. As you can imagine, it makes me a tiny bit less sad when I have to pay for a burst septic tank if at least I know I'm a little closer to a first-class upgrade on my next trip.

Cherish ♫ Your Checklist ♫

Before you celebrate your first rent check, make sure you're prepared for the stuff no one likes to think about. Let's review your start-up financial checklist:

- Set aside three to six months of property expenses (mortgage, taxes, insurance, utilities, HOA)
- Create a repair & maintenance fund of at least 1–2% of the property value per year
- Have your CapEx fund set up and ready for emergencies. If you are just starting, put any excess rental income here so you are not in a jam later.

Plan for property maintenance. Be prepared for both major and minor maintenance items such as:

- HVAC servicing & repair
- Water heater replacement
- Refrigerator & major appliances
- Plumbing issues (clogs, leaks, backups)
- Roof patches or replacement (especially for older homes)
- Turnover cleaning
- Pest control
- Basic handyman work
- Furniture wear and tear for furnished homes (yes, someone *will* jump on your couch)

While this chapter is focused on long-term rentals, these maintenance items will apply to almost all real estate, whether it's a long-term rental, short-term rental, multi-family, etc. If you own a property that has a roof, plumbing, electricity, etc., you need to be prepared to maintain and update it.

Managing All That Cash

Set up a separate bank account for each rental property. This isn't just about organization—it's about protection. When you keep your property finances separate, you avoid *commingling funds* which can create legal and accounting headaches later. If your properties are owned under an LLC or other business entity, mixing personal and property money can actually pierce the corporate veil—meaning you could lose the liability protection that keeps your personal assets safe if something goes wrong.

Keeping every rental's income and expenses in its own account also makes it crystal clear how each property is performing. You'll instantly know your true profit, your reserves, and what needs attention.

> **ROCKSTAR TIP**
> Set up a separate bank account for each rental property. Automate transfers to pay bills and add to reserves.

Automating transfers for your mortgage, bills, and reserves builds consistency and peace of mind—you're protecting your business, your personal finances, and your future.

This simple system creates both financial clarity and legal security. Treat each property like a business from day one, and you'll not only build wealth—you'll protect it like the Boss Lady you are.

Manage Like a Boss
♫ *Who's That Girl?* ♫

New investors often ask if they should self-manage their properties. Maybe at first. That will depend on several factors, a major one being if you have the time to manage. If not, hire a property manager (and make sure to calculate that into your numbers). If you can and want to manage your own rentals, it's a great way to learn the ins and outs of all things rental.

You'll learn to handle:

- Marketing the property
- Screening tenants
- Collecting rent
- Scheduling repairs

This will help you later as you build and grow, while providing you with a foundation of understanding. But, once you have more than a few properties, consider a property manager. They will take a lot of the burden off your shoulders. It can be hard to let go, but you can't grow if you are spending all your time managing. The property manager can take away the headaches so you can get to building your portfolio.

As women, we have a hard time letting go. Trust me, when I first got started, I managed everything on my own—the maintenance calls, the late-night texts from tenants, the cleanings, the repairs. I didn't want to let go. I was afraid nobody would care as much as I did.

Eventually, the workload demanded that I bring on help. As it turned out, having help enabled me to spend more time doing the things I enjoyed and less time on things I did not (the 2:00 am phone calls in particular). As my portfolio grew, that help turned into something much bigger: I founded my own property management company. Now, my properties are managed *by* that company, with a professional team handling the day-to-day.

Here's the scoop. You don't need to do it all yourself to be a great investor. In fact, in many cases, it makes *way* more sense to hire a manager. For some of you, this may even be at the very beginning. Maybe you have a full-time job. Perhaps you can't deal with tenant issues like toilet emergencies *even* in the middle of the day. Maybe you travel frequently, live out of state, or are only interested in passive investing. That's not a weakness; it's a smart strategy. A great property manager can help maximize your profits, reduce your stress, and make your investment *feel* like an investment rather than another "job."

Whether you DIY or outsource, the key is to know your limits, understand your numbers, and choose what aligns best with your lifestyle and goals. There's no one "right" way, only the way that works for *you.*

Protect Your Assets
♬ *Die Another Day* ♬

This is the step many people forget. It can cost you big.

The last thing you want is to do the work, start growing your assets and then have something happen that puts it all at risk. There are some key strategies to making sure you and your assets are protected.

First, make sure you have the right type *and* the right amount of insurance coverage. For rentals, this won't be your standard homeowner's insurance policy. There are several types of insurance that you will want to consider. Choose the one that works for your situation. That could be landlord insurance, vacation rental insurance, general liability or some other type of coverage. These protections will cover you in the event of loss of rent, tenant damage, or liability claims. It's your safety net. Shop and compare rates but choose the coverage that protects you best.

Make sure your tenants understand that their belongings aren't covered if something happens to the home: fire, flood, hurricane, anything. Require renter's insurance to protect their personal property.

Next, protect the asset legally. Consider putting the property in an LLC or setting up an umbrella policy, which is extra liability insurance that kicks in when the limits of your homeowners, auto, or rental property insurance aren't enough. Think of it like a financial safety net that protects your assets —your savings, investments, and even future income, if something big happens, like a major accident or lawsuit.

For example, if someone gets hurt at your rental property and sues for more than your regular policy covers, your umbrella policy "opens up" to cover the difference. It's surprisingly affordable for the amount of protection it provides and is a smart move for any Boss Lady building wealth and protecting what she's worked hard for.

Every investor's situation is different. Consult a CPA or real estate attorney who understands landlord asset protection and tax law. You're not just growing your wealth; you're building a fortress.

Lastly, consider estate planning. If something happens to you, what happens to your properties? A living trust or clear succession plan ensures your investments keep serving your family long after you're gone.

You've worked hard to build your empire, so protect it like the Boss Lady you are.

We've made it to the good stuff. You're ready to buy your first rental property.

Maybe you've already found a cute little gem that's rent-ready. Hopefully the numbers make your spreadsheet do a happy dance. In that case? Buy that sucker and get to landlady-ing. But let me rewind and spill some real-life tea on how this all started for me.

Grow
♫ Over and Over ♫

If, like me, your goal isn't one rental forever but rather a portfolio that buys back your freedom, your first property is *the step* to get you closer to that goal. Above and beyond getting you motivated and earning you extra dough, your first property can become the catalyst to fund your next property. And then the next.

How? Let me explain.

- Let House #1 build equity.
- Use the equity to buy House #2 (refinancing)
- Repeat.

Or, should you decide to update or renovate the home, you may be able to refinance the property and reclaim your cash.

Many investors rinse and repeat until they have five, ten, twenty or even more homes. Each one adds cash flow and wealth.

I bought my first intentional long-term rental with just as much anxiety about it as the next gal. But if I wanted to grow, I had to start somewhere. Back then, I didn't have a lot to work with. Don't let that stop you. Don't get analysis paralysis.

Do *get started*! We'll go deeper into how to scale your empire a little later in the book.

BRRRR: A Boss Lady Strategy

If you started learning about real estate investing prior to this book, you have likely heard of BRRRR. If you've never heard of it, it's not about a cold plunge to freeze away your stress (though there is huge value in that type of brrrr, too). Real estate BRRRR (Buy, Rehab, Rent, Refinance, Repeat) is not just a catchy acronym. It's the ultimate playbook for Boss Ladies looking to build wealth strategically—and multiply it.

It's also a mindset. It's when you stop *looking* for the perfect property and start *creating* it. It's where you don't worry about if a property is cute today and start focusing on what the math says for tomorrow. BRRRR is the shift from consumer to creator. From buyer to investor. From paycheck-to-paycheck to wealth-on-repeat.

🎶 Burning Up 🎶
The BRRRR

The BRRRR method follows the same steps we just went through except with the BRRRR method you will intentionally look for a house that has an *unrealized* built in value. That could be a home that is dated and needs modernization or one with a strange layout that could be reconfigured to be more user-friendly. There could be an opportunity for a new bedroom to be added with a new layout. Whatever it is, with the BRRRR you will want to find a property that you can add value to *with renovations*.

The BRRRR Strategy

Buy
Renovate
Rent
Refinance
Repeat

Here's how BRRRR works:

Step 1. Buy a Property

You identify the area you want to invest in. A house comes on the market, but it has issues. It's not turnkey—it has a dated kitchen, a funky layout, or shag carpet straight out of 1976. There must be something about the property that you can improve to make it worth significantly more than its current price.

You get the house under contract for a great deal and have your team ready—contractors, lender, realtor, insurance agent, everyone lined up. Then comes financing. Instead of a conventional loan (which usually won't fund fixer-uppers or cover rehab costs), you'll likely use hard money, a HELOC, or a DSCR loan.

We will cover these in more depth in Chapters 7 and 8, but these financing tools are designed for investors who need speed and flexibility. Hard-money loans are short-term and fast to close, perfect for properties that need major work. A HELOC lets you tap into the equity of another property to fund the renovation. And a DSCR loan focuses on the property's income potential rather than your personal income, making it ideal if you're building a rental portfolio.

Each of these loan types helps you move quickly, take advantage of deals others can't, and build equity fast—key ingredients in a successful BRRRR strategy.

You close on (purchase) the house. This is the B in BRRRR. BUY.

Step 2. Make Renovations

Now the renovations start, the first R in BRRRR. RENOVATE or REHAB.

Step 3. Rent the Property

Once the house is renovated, it's ready for a new tenant to move into. You've made it up-to-date and all major items (roof, a/c, etc.) are new or newer. With the house looking so nice, you suddenly have a slew of tenant applications. This is the second R in BRRRR. RENT.

Step 4. Refinance

Now you go to a conventional mortgage lender. You are still paying the hard money loan, but now you can show the bank lender that the house is worth more post-rehab, and you have rental income from your tenant. At this point, the bank will likely give you a loan, so you do the third R in BRRRR and you REFINANCE.

But wait—here's where the secret sauce is. When you refinance, you are aiming to get most or all your money back. What do I mean? Let's look at the numbers.

Let's say you find an older two-bedroom, two-bath home with good bones for a decent price. The kitchen and bathrooms are dated, and there is a strange addition off the back of the house, but it's in a decent neighborhood with strong rental potential.

Because of how outdated the home is, you can negotiate a great deal on the house. For example, let's say $200,000. In this instance, you get a $180,000 DSCR loan. You still have to put down 10% ($20,000) of your personal money to secure the loan. That means, so far, you have personally contributed $20,000; the rest is someone else's money.

You'll need to spend another $70,000 renovating the kitchen and bathrooms, painting the interior and replacing old carpets with vinyl planks. You turn the weird back room into a third bedroom.

Where do you get the $70,000? You get a HELOC on your primary residence because, like a Boss Lady, you have built up the equity by paying down your mortgage.

The house is now an updated 3-bedroom 2-bath home. You get a renter almost immediately for $3,000/mo.

You go to the bank and show them your renovations and the lease. The bank sends their appraiser out and now, with the updates, the house appraises at $350,000.

Don't forget, even when you refinance, the bank will only finance 80% of the value ($280,000).

How much money do *you* have in this investment now?

> DSCR + HELOC: $250,000 ($180,000 + $70,000)
> Personal investment: $20,000
> Refinance amount available: $280,000

This means the bank is willing to give you $10,000 *more* than you paid in the first place! Ladies, don't be foolish here and take more than you need. Take the loan for $270,000 to pay off the higher interest DSCR loan and HELOC, and pay yourself back your $20,000 investment. You now have zero dollars invested in the property. Every dollar invested now comes from the bank in the form of a loan. Your tenants will be the ones paying the loan through rent.

Boom!

You now have $80,000 in equity and monthly rental income which you use to pay down the mortgage, plus a little extra to put in your pocket. And let's repeat ... you now have zero personal dollars invested. That's what I call a Boss Lady move!

Step 5. Repeat

Which leads us to our final R in BRRRR ... REPEAT.

You can see why investors love the BRRRR method—it's simple, easy and duplicatable.

Want an added boost to make this even sweeter?

Owning a rental property isn't just about collecting monthly rent; it's about working smarter come tax season. On top of building your wealth and portfolio, the IRS also gives investors all kinds of goodies. With rental properties, you get to:

- Deduct mortgage interest, taxes, insurance, repairs
- Deduct travel and management expenses
- Depreciate the property over time, even if it's going up in value

This is like getting rewarded for owning an appreciating asset.

And the cherry on top when you're ready to sell? Use a 1031 Exchange to roll your profits into another property *without paying capital gains taxes* right away. That's next-level wealth building.

What Is a 1031 Exchange?

A 1031 Exchange (named after Section 1031 of the IRS Code) lets real estate investors sell one investment property and reinvest the profits into another "like-kind" property—without paying capital gains taxes at the time of sale. It's one of the most powerful tools in real estate for building long-term wealth and growing your portfolio faster.

You can use a 1031 Exchange for almost any type of investment property—long-term rentals, short-term vacation rentals, or multi-family properties—as long as you follow IRS guidelines and the properties are both held for investment or business purposes (not for personal use).

Think of a 1031 Exchange as a tax-deferred upgrade: you sell one property, roll the profits into your next deal, and keep your money working for you instead of handing it over to the IRS. We'll dig deeper later in Chapter 8 on how to structure one properly and avoid common mistakes.

The tax code was written with investors in mind. You just must know how to play the game. Don't skip this step, get a good CPA, and treat your real estate like the business it is.

> **ROCKSTAR TIP**
>
> Use a 1031 Exchange to sell one property, defer the tax, and keep your money working for you.

Rehabbing and construction not your jam?

The BRRRR method isn't for everyone, and it isn't for every deal. Don't worry, rehabs aren't required to make money in real estate investing. About half my portfolio didn't need a full remodel. Sometimes deals can be found in well-priced, clean properties that you can rent out as-is, some are purchased completely turnkey after someone else has done the rehab. If the numbers make sense, go for it.

I once bought a $122,500 bungalow. We put $24,500 down. Rented it for $1,200/month. Two years later, it appraised for $175,000. We refinanced, pulled out our equity, and kept rolling.

Sometimes, slow and steady builds just as much wealth as the flashier flips.

This journey isn't always as smooth as it can sound. I've had a septic tank explode. I've gone over budget. I've had DEA agents surround a house while tenants jumped out of windows. Wild. But the rent still came. The equity still built. The wealth still compounded.

From foreclosure to financial freedom, the BRRRR method changed my life. It can change yours too.

Buy smart. Rehab with vision. Rent with care. Refinance with confidence. Repeat with joy.

You've got this, Boss Lady. Let's build your empire.

Long-term rentals are not overnight jackpots. They're slow-burn wealth. You'll have boring months. Unexpected repairs. Tenant drama.

But you'll also have steady checks. Tax benefits. Growing equity. And the deep satisfaction of knowing *your money works harder than you do.*

Stay the course. Breathe through the headaches. Celebrate the wins.

Habits of a
♫ Superstar ♫

Many of my lessons didn't come from a textbook, they came from trenches, tears, and triumphs. If I could sit you down with a glass of wine and drop some real estate wisdom on you, here's what I'd share:

Know Your Paperwork Like a Pro

Carefully read all the closing documents I described earlier in this chapter. I once found an error before closing that saved me $1,400, just because I took the time to double-check the prorations for taxes and insurance.

When you're at the closing table, don't just nod along, ask questions. If you're just starting out, have the closing attorney or title rep walk you through each section. Ask what you don't understand. Seriously, don't be shy. There is *no shame* in asking smart questions. The more you know, the more confidently you'll sign that dotted line and the more money you'll keep in your pocket.

Treat Your Dream Team Like Gold

In Chapter 2, I talked about building your Dream Team—your bankers, contractors, mortgage brokers, inspectors and others. Relationships are everything in this game. They're your lifelines; keep them close. If they engage actively at Chamber of Commerce events, volunteer in the community, or sponsor local causes, join them. Be present.

Send thank-you cards. Remember birthdays. Treat them like the VIPs they are. Because when you show up with gratitude and professionalism, you'll find your offers getting priority, your bids getting noticed, and people bending over backwards to help when things go sideways (and they *will* go sideways). You're not just building a portfolio; you're building a tribe.

Stay on top of Construction Costs

Estimating renovation costs is an art. It takes time to learn all "the things." I still get nervous every time I bid. Just today, I lost an auction and felt relieved because I wasn't sure if my reno estimates were right! But that's part of the process—you learn, you evolve.

Start by talking to multiple contractors. Ask questions. Visit job sites. Study past project breakdowns. I'm constantly reviewing bids, reading receipts, and yes ... Googling. Not because the internet is always right, but because it helps me spot red flags or outrageous pricing. You don't have to be a general contractor, but you *do* need to understand enough to protect your budget and your bottom line.

House Hacking: The Smartest Start to Building Equity

If you're just getting started in real estate and don't have piles of cash sitting around, I have one word for you: house hacking. (Ok, that's two words). It's one of the most powerful, practical, and creative ways to start building equity and cash flow with minimal money down. It's not flashy, but it's smart, and smart is what gets you rich.

What Is House Hacking?

House hacking is buying a property and living in part of it while renting out the rest to offset or even eliminate your housing costs. Think duplex, triplex, or a single-family home with rentable space like a guest suite, finished basement, or even extra bedrooms. The goal is simple: let other people's rent payments help cover your mortgage while you build equity.

For example, you might buy a duplex for $350,000. You live in one unit and rent out the other for $1,500 per month. If your total mortgage, taxes, and insurance are $2,000, you're now only paying $500 a month to live there. That's less than most car payments, and you're investing, not spending.

Previously, in *Becoming a Boss Lady Investor* ...

In my first book, *Becoming a Boss Lady Investor*, I shared how my husband pulled off one of the smartest money moves I've ever seen, before we even met. (Side note: who you marry or partner with will absolutely impact your financial life, so choose wisely!)

That experience opened my eyes to just how powerful house hacking can be, especially for anyone getting started in real estate with limited cash. Watching Colin turn a starter home into a long-term wealth builder proved that you don't have to start big to think like an investor. You just need creativity, a willingness to share your space, and a little grit.

We're going to revisit my husband's story and look at what would have happened if he *hadn't* house-hacked. You'll see why this strategy can completely change your financial future.

Real-Life Example: My Husband's "Frat House" Hack

Before we were married, my husband bought a townhouse for about $180,000. His mortgage payment was around $1,100 per month, and instead of shouldering that whole cost alone, he rented out two rooms to his buddies for $500 each, including utilities and internet. That brought in $1,000 a month, leaving him to cover just $100 plus utilities.

He lived there for four years, basically hanging out with his friends, living almost rent-free, and building equity. When we decided to move in together, he kept the townhouse as a rental property (since we were underwater on it) and leased the entire home for $1,200 per month.

During the Great Recession, we sometimes paid out of pocket about $200 a month to keep it going. Trust me, during those tough years, that extra $200 felt like a big deal. Over the next seven years, we paid about $4,800 out of pocket, not something either of us loved doing. But, when we sold it, we actually made over $50,000 in net profit. That's an incredible return for what was essentially a house he lived in with friends.

The lesson? Even when things feel tight, sticking with your investment can pay off big in the long run.

What If He Hadn't House-Hacked?

To really understand the power of house hacking, let's look at what would have happened if Colin had made different choices.

If he had rented: He would have spent around $43,200 over four years on rent before we moved in together and walked away with zero equity, zero tax benefits, and zero profit. That money would have gone straight into someone else's pocket.

If he had bought, but lived alone: His total cost of living and maintaining the home would have been around $57,600 over eleven years. After selling for a $60,000 profit, he would have basically broken even after over a decade of effort.

But because he house hacked: His total cost was about $9,600 across eleven years, and he sold for a $60,000 profit. That's a $50,000+ net win, and he lived almost rent-free the entire time he lived in the townhouse.

Scenario	11-Yr Out-of-Pocket	Profit From Sale	Net Result
Rent	$57,600	none	$57,600 (loss)
Buy & Live Alone	$57,600	$60,000	$2,400 (break-even)
Buy & House Hack	$9,600	$60,000	$50,000 (profit)

Boss Lady Takeaway: House hacking turned a normal 20-something just trying to afford his mortgage into an investor. Simply by sharing his space, Colin saved over $50,000 compared to renting or living alone. (Marrying me was the bonus). Those savings became the foundation for our next investments, and that's how wealth starts to snowball.

Our Florida Guest Cottage: The Cutest House Hack Ever

Fast forward to today, our home in Florida has a guest cottage on the property. We decorated it super cute (of course!) and turned it into a short-term vacation rental. It brings in about $1,200 a month, which we use to pay down the principal on our mortgage.

You can do this too!

Let's say you own a home worth $600,000 with a 30-year mortgage at 6.5% interest. Your monthly principal and interest payment would be around $3,792 (not including taxes and insurance).

Now imagine you rent out a guest suite, small cottage, or even a camper parked on your property for $1,000 per month and you apply that income directly to your loan's principal each month.

Here's where the magic happens:

- Without the extra payments, your mortgage would take 30 years to pay off.
- By putting an extra $1,000 a month toward the principal, you would pay the home off in about *16 years instead of 30.*
- You'd also *save roughly $280,000 in interest over the life of the loan.*

That's not just shaving off a few years, it's cutting your mortgage in *half* and freeing yourself from nearly an extra decade and a half of payments.

So, whether you have a guest cottage, converted garage, RV, or cozy mother-in-law suite, using that rental income strategically can fast-track your financial freedom. Even one renter can change the entire trajectory of your wealth.

Don't think of that $1,000 as "extra spending money." Think of it as an accelerator pedal for your equity. Every dollar you throw at principal is a dollar you'll never pay interest on again.

> **ROCKSTAR TIP**
> Use the income from house hacking to pay down the principal on your mortgage.

Here's where we made it even sweeter. At the same time we started renting out the guest cottage, my bestie (and business partner!) was between homes, so she lived with us for two years. She paid $800 a month, which we also applied straight to our mortgage principal. That extra payment alone will shorten the loan by about five additional years and save tens of thousands in interest.

It's a win-win: she got a beautiful place to live on the water, and we built equity faster without even noticing the extra money leaving our account.

Other Ways Boss Ladies Are Hacking the System

My editor used the same approach, but instead of using the rental income to pay down her mortgage, she uses her guest house for extra retirement cash flow. Every month, that little rental brings in fun money she can use for travel, hobbies, or spoiling her grandkids.

And my parents? They were the original house hackers before the term even existed. They got married at 18 (OMG, so young!) and bought a small townhouse. They were broke, but they rented out one side while living in the other. That rental income was the only way they could afford to own anything at all. They lived there until they built up some savings, then sold the property and bought their own home. That's generational Boss Lady thinking right there.

Modern Twists on House Hacking

House hacking has evolved far beyond duplexes and basements. These days, people rent out:

- Guest suites, RVs, or ADUs (accessory dwelling units) on their property
- Rooms in their primary home to traveling nurses or students
- Their entire house when they go on extended trips
- Or even do international house swaps (I've been offered a month in Portugal in exchange for someone staying at my Florida home—how fun is that?)

Not all hacks are financial; some are experiential. Instead of paying for a hotel abroad, you can trade homes and experiences while your place earns its keep.

Know Your Comfort Zone

That said, house hacking isn't for everyone, and that's okay. When I was a young single mom, the idea of renting out a room to strangers would've freaked me out. Safety always comes first, and you have to honor your comfort level and family's boundaries. There will be seasons in life when house hacking makes perfect sense, and others when it just doesn't fit.

But if it *does* fit? Lean in. This strategy can be one of the most powerful ways to accelerate your path to financial freedom. It's flexible, creative, and proven and I still look for ways to incorporate it into my life to this day.

Boss Lady Takeaway: House hacking isn't just a strategy, it's a mindset. It's about thinking smarter with what you already have, making your home work for you, and using creativity (and a little grit) to build long-term wealth.

Your Legacy Starts Here
♫ *Take a Bow* ♫

Before you turn the page ...

I've created custom worksheets just for you, and trust me, they're more than just busywork. They are where you take everything we just covered and start putting it into action. You can download several worksheets free (because I love you) or you can buy the complete workbook on my website, www.thebossladyinvestor.com.

Take the time to complete them thoughtfully. Save copies so you can revisit and reuse it for future deals (because spoiler alert: there *will* be more!). I recommend completing the steps I gave you and working through the worksheets before moving on to the next chapter.

Why? Because once you're knee-deep in new info, it's easy to forget what you've just learned. And this stuff? This is foundational.

Pause, do the work, and then dive back in, knowing you're not just reading about becoming a real estate investor, you're *doing* it.

Boss Lady, this is how you build generational wealth. It's how you pay for your kids' college without loans, retire early, or spend three months a year traveling Europe.

One rental at a time. Boring? Maybe. But dependable? Always.

Grab that "classic purse" property and watch what happens when you bet on YOU.

Let's go, Boss Lady.

Chapter 4
VACATION RENTALS

From Rock Bottom to Beachfront Boss Lady
♬ *Something in the Water* ♬

Imagine waking up, sipping your morning latte in fuzzy slippers, and checking your phone to find out you just made $742 *while you slept.*

And no, you're not dreaming. You're just a vacation rental owner now, babe.

Whether it's a cozy mountain cabin, a chic condo by the beach, or a desert escape with a hot tub under the stars, investing in short-term rentals (STRs) is one of the most *fabulous* ways to build wealth *and* create a lifestyle you love. It's like real estate investing but with more throw pillows and Instagrammable sunset views.

This chapter is your go-to guide for stepping into the vacation rental game like the Boss Lady you are.

The Basics

Let's break it down: vacation rentals (aka short-term rentals or STRs) are properties rented out on platforms like Airbnb, VRBO, or even directly to guests. Think of it as the real estate version of a capsule wardrobe: minimal risk, max versatility, and serious money potential.

Here's why Boss Ladies like me LOVE vacation rentals:

Higher income potential. STRs often earn 2–3x what a long-term rental does.

Personal use. Hello, free vacation home!

Tax perks. Yes, Queen—vacation rentals come with sweet deductions.

Creative freedom. Design it, brand it, make it yours! The first time I stayed in a vacation rental, I wasn't scouting an investment opportunity, I was running away. More about that in a bit.

Vacation Rentals Are the ♫ *It Girl* ♫

If long-term rentals are your go-to Coach bag, vacation rentals are your Gucci.

Flashier, high-maintenance, and a head-turner. Vacation rentals require more hands-on attention, but the returns, and the Instagram-worthy aesthetics, are next-level. A vacation rental home can be a wonderfully smart investment, just one that comes with a bit more flair, a bit more involvement and thus, a bit more risk.

How do you get into vacation rental investing? For me, the dream started years before the reality happened ... but hey, what good story doesn't start with a dream?

It was during my second marriage. Life felt like a beautiful, well-decorated dumpster fire. Needing to get away from the constant arguing at home, I took a leap of faith and joined my tennis team on a lady's tennis trip to Amelia Island, hoping salty air and sunshine would drown out the sound of my collapsing marriage. I had recently joined the team, so I drove there solo instead of with the crew. (I'm the type that needs an "escape route" even if I don't use it). I wasn't sure what to expect when I made my way to the outskirts of the sleepy little beach town. My directions led to a charming house right across from the ocean. The moment I stepped inside, I was hooked.

This place wasn't just four walls and a roof—it felt like a *hug.* It was light, airy, dotted with adorable coastal décor, clean as a whistle, and dripping with personality. Even the cheesy bathroom signs made me smile. It was obvious: someone *cared* about this place. Someone made it a home for *strangers.*

As it turned out, it belonged to my tennis partner's aunt, a single woman who somehow owned this adorable seaside vacation rental *plus* she owned her primary residence back in Atlanta. Though I had never met her, she was my personal shero: smart, independent, financially free. A few days into the trip, while standing barefoot on the front porch with sand still on my toes, I thought: *One day, I'm going to have a vacation home. One day, I will stand on my front porch listening to ocean waves roll in.*

It felt impossible back then. Life for me had been hard, nothing seemed to come easy and just making my mortgage payment was often a struggle. Add to that the obvious failure of my *second* marriage and you can rightfully assume my self-esteem was teetering on the brink of extinction. But luckily (and thanks to a lot of prayer and deep soul searching) I hadn't lost my will to dream.

On that particular day, I was smiling from the inside out. My friends and I had a fabulous day on the beach boogie boarding (where I had my own Janet Jackson moment), spent the afternoon dining on a delicious fresh catch lunch and enjoyed girl time that had us laughing until our sides hurt (those are the best).

That weekend was the perfect place for me to regroup and find joy. Surrounding myself with a group of positive and uplifting women reminded me that I had value and was worthy of dreaming. I doubt that group of ladies will ever know what they did for me in that moment of my life, but they made me remember who I was. Being around them restored a piece of me. Being in that house reminded me that there are driven people all around the world making things happen. If they could do it, so could I.

Fortunately, that wide-eyed twenty-something me loving that moment, didn't know that my marriage would implode less than a year after that trip. This was before life, and some not-so-great fiscal choices, led me to my financial rock bottom which included a foreclosure, bankruptcy, and lots, I mean *lots,* of tears. Yet somehow, even with all that, I held onto the dream of something bigger more tightly than my favorite tennis racket.

Eight years later, my dream became a reality.

Buying the Beach House: Sweat, Grit, and a Ton of ♫ Dirty Laundry ♫

I was still living in Atlanta when I bought my first beach house. By then, I was married to my third (and final) husband. This time, my relationship was healthy, supportive and loving. It's not surprising that when you are in a healthy relationship, other parts of your life become stronger, too. I was mentally, physically and financially growing. Though I had gotten myself back on solid financial footing, having a partner that was supportive and uplifting certainly changed the game. To be clear, you don't need a partner to be a Boss Lady real estate investor. But if you do have a partner, they need to be supportive and part of your team, or it simply won't work.

Colin and I were in a strong financial spot, our jobs were going well, the bills were paid and we were saving money. My credit was still damaged from the bankruptcy, but through the years it was rebuilding and getting better. His credit was strong. We didn't have any major debts.

Luckily, even before Amazon, Temu or Shien, I have always been a thrifty shopper. Spending large amounts of money on things that are trivial (to me) isn't my jam. Now that I had money in the bank, I could spend freely on things that caught my eye. Things that would, over time, chip away at our savings. But I didn't.

Sadly, I see it happen all the time. A promotion, commission or bonus check is used to buy a lavish trip, fancy car or a designer handbag. Then years, or maybe only months later, the money is gone with no wealth building to show for it.

Don't get me wrong. I'm not saying don't have fun. I'm saying if you want to create lasting wealth, you must make hard choices. Walking away from luxury purchases is another superpower of a Boss Lady real estate investor, and it's one that you will need to learn to grow true wealth.

I was in a financial era where for me a Louis Vuitton purse would have been a significant purchase; and girl, I'm telling you, I really wanted a fancy purse. Even when we finally had a lump of money sitting in the bank, it took everything in me not to go blazing through the Mall of Georgia like a Kardashian.

Purses, shoes, super cute outfits—yes please! It would have been so easy to do.

But I didn't.

Because by then, I thoroughly understood the consequences of bad financial behavior. If, like me, you go through fire, at least learn the lessons along the way so you don't burn yourself again.

So, instead of the Gucci sunglasses or LV bag (which I'm sure would have made me look like a rockstar), we decided to invest our money. No mall shopping spree for this newly budding boss lady.

The investment? A house at the beach.

The dream was finally becoming a reality.

Sort of.

Unlike my friend's aunt's beach house, ours was a little more, shall we say, "rustic". It wasn't fancy by any stretch of the imagination, but it had a pool and was five glorious minutes from the ocean. By not fancy, I mean there was no insulation, drop ceilings (yes, like the kind you had in your classrooms growing up), wallpaper so thick we had to use knives to cut through it and two tiny, outdated bathrooms.

But to me it was heaven. Or at least, my personal sanctuary that I could drive to every weekend for some much-needed Vitamin-Sea (and D).

Initially, we bought the house for our own use, we weren't planning to rent it out. At the time, cash flow wasn't my number one priority (I was still learning back then) so we were banking on the home appreciating over the years. But after a few trips and realizing that it would be vacant pretty frequently, we decided to see what would happen if we tried to rent it out.

The deal looked like this:

VACATION RENTAL #1	
Purchase Price	196,000
Down Payment	50,000
Mortgage Payment /mo	716
Taxes /year	5,000
Insurance /year	4,000
Furniture & Décor	10,000
Renovations	20,000

Before you start thinking, *"There's no way you can buy a beach house for $196,000,"* let me stop you.

This was back in 2014, and at the time that price felt like a huge leap for me. The Great Recession had only recently loosened its grip, and housing prices were still depressed. That downturn turned out to be a blessing in disguise, but at that moment very few people were confidently snapping up second homes.

Here's the lesson: markets rise and fall. The smartest Boss Ladies know that if a property has good cash flow in a down market, the sky's the limit when the market swings up.

But the numbers need to make sense for your situation, and if they don't, don't force it.

Keep saving until you can put enough down to make the property produce a positive cash flow, wait for interest rates to drop, or pivot to a different house. Your power as an investor is your ability to adjust and move with the market, never against it.

Once we closed on our beach house, I made our renovation and décor budget stretch further than yoga pants on Thanksgiving. Clearance deals, flea markets, garage sales—you name it, I hunted it. Friends who thought they were coming for a beach weekend found themselves holding paintbrushes and crowbars.

Years later, I would understand that we should have put more money into the renovation and less towards the down payment, but you live, and you learn. I'll explain more about that later.

We did much of the renovation work ourselves. Hiring a crew was out of our budget. My girlfriends and I had crafting and painting parties at the beach where we created ocean-themed décor by day and sipped cocktails by the pool at night. My décor may not be fancy, but it is original, exists *only* in my home and reminds me of cherished memories.

Sweat equity was all we had. Looking back, that home is still one of my most fulfilling renovations.

Three months later we posted the home on Airbnb. I held my breath and prayed for bookings. *Please, universe. Let people love it as much as I do.*

My hubby and I were full of nervous anticipation. We'd never owned a home in another state. Airbnb was relatively new. We didn't have a housekeeper. We didn't know what we didn't know (like the kind of insurance we needed or how to set pricing). Maybe we aren't the premier example of how to start your first vacation rental, but hey, we got started. *Done is better than perfect*, thanks Brené.

It was magic. In the first year we generated over $100,000 in gross revenue, and $42,800 in rental income.

You read that right. Over $42,000!

VACATION RENTAL #1		
INVESTMENT		
Purchase price	196,000	
FUNDING (Conv. Mortgage)		
Down Payment	50,000	
Mortgage Amount	146,000	
Interest Rate	4.125%	
FIRST YEAR REVENUE		100,000
FIRST YEAR EXPENSES		
Renovations	(20,000)	
Furniture & Décor	(10,000)	
Mortgage Payment	(8,592)	
Taxes	(5,000)	
Insurance	(4,000)	
Utilities & Maintenance	(9,600)	
Expense Total:		(57,192)
FIRST YEAR CASH FLOW		42,808

Yes, we did eventually find a great housekeeper, get the right insurance and learn how to structure pricing, but that didn't happen overnight. There were plenty of mistakes made along the way. Refunds were given. Guests showed up to houses that the cleaner had never cleaned. All these things had me questioning my decision, wondering if I should quit. But instead of quitting, I took the lessons and learned. Hopefully, with the help of this book, you will have fewer struggles from the get-go.

We also made lots of good decisions, and *so will you.* Throughout your journey, there will be moments when you doubt yourself. Breathe in and "do it by the book". This book is giving you the freedom to do it imperfectly. Just do it! That first investment opened a world that would change my life. Yours will too, you just need the courage to jump.

We could have avoided the costly mistakes made during renovations. We could have avoided the headaches that come with rentals. I could have bought the handbag. But what would we have today?

A worn purse, old shoes and fancy clothing that would hopefully come back in style one day.

Instead, we built an empire.

That single house would yield us hundreds of thousands of dollars in rental revenue. We still own the home, and today it's worth way more than what we paid. When we cash out (which we plan to do after twenty years), we will have realized close to a million dollars in gains.

These days, I can buy the fancy purse without batting a perfectly curled eyelash. If I'm being honest, that's still not my jam, although I am guilty of owning a few cute bags. What I do spend my excess money on now is cruising the Nile River through Egypt, going on safari with my family in Africa, exploring ancient ruins in Peru, surfing the waves of Portugal and enjoying yummy delights in Croatia. I can live life on my terms, knowing the rent checks will still come, no matter where I may be in the world.

You don't have to be rich before buying the beach house; in fact, the beach house may help make you rich. But you will have to be resourceful, educated and gritty.

Now that I had proof of concept, it was time to scale.

I'm going to walk you through our first several rentals and then we will review the steps you need to take to enter this exciting field of investing.

Scaling Up After Starting
♬ So Small ♬

Vacation Rental 2: Family Partnership + HELOC Magic

Six months later, high on success and a bit too much optimism, I bought my second vacation rental. This time the house I had my eye on was in foreclosure and would require a full cash payment to purchase.

While I was doing pretty good, I certainly didn't have a spare $200,000 sitting in the bank.

So, I partnered with my cousin. She was in a different situation than I was and paid cash for her portion. I tapped a Home Equity Line of Credit (HELOC) from my primary residence. With this combo, we were able to purchase the home for cash. We split the costs, shared the profits, and I added to my beachside empire.

I want to stop here for a minute and discuss an often-misunderstood concept.

Above, I stated both that I took a home equity line of credit (which is a debt/loan) AND that we purchased the home for cash. How does that even make sense?

When someone says, "I paid cash for this house," twenty-year old me believed that to mean they had saved up all their pennies and then one day had enough to write a check or pay greenbacks to buy the home.

WRONG.

A much older me now understands that "paying cash" doesn't necessarily mean you pay cash (though some people actually do). Huh? Weird, I know. What it does mean, is that you paid the seller in cash. It means that the purchase of the home wasn't contingent on you obtaining a mortgage.

Because this deserves much more detail, and I don't want to get off track on our vacation home process, we will dive more deeply into the "cash purchase" in Chapter 7 when we go into the details of funding options.

Back to Vacation Rental 2.

A few years after our purchase, my cousin ran into a jam (aka her own divorce), so my husband and I bought her out and then cash-out refinanced the home.

A cash-out refinance lets you replace your existing mortgage with a new, larger one and take the difference out in cash—essentially tapping into your home's equity to fund your next investment or renovation. We'll dive deeper into how and when to use this powerful wealth-building tool later in the book.

Vacation rental laws, zoning and regulations changed a few years later, and we eventually turned the home into a traditional long-term rental, but let's break down the numbers before that happened. Don't worry, I'll give you the long-term rental numbers, too.

Vacation Rental 2 was a beach house, just a 10-minute walk to the beach. It had four bedrooms, two bathrooms, and one pool. The pool is important. Why?

> **ROCKSTAR TIP**
> In vacation areas, know which amenities drive bookings and income.

In vacation areas, amenities drive bookings and income. In Florida, a pool is gold—it boosts occupancy and nightly rates enough to easily cover its cost and upkeep. The same goes for ski destinations, where ski-in/ski-out access or hot tubs can make your property stand out and earn more.

The deal looked like this:

VACATION RENTAL #2		
	Full Amt.	**50%**
Purchase Price	190,000	95,000
Utilities /mo		400
HELOC Payment /mo		750
Taxes /mo		187
Insurance /mo		208
Furniture & Décor	15,000	7,500
Renovations	30,000	15,000

The purchase price was $190,000. My portion would only be half, so my purchase price was $95,000. My cousin paid for the other half.

We invested $30,000 in renovations. We renovated both bathrooms, added a new A/C, hot water heater and pool pump. We paid a contractor for those items, but we painted the walls, replaced lighting, curtain rods and ceiling fans. Doing some of the work saved us quite a bit of cash.

I paid for my loan and my portion of the renovations using funds from my HELOC. My total HELOC loan was $110,000 ($95,000 purchase price plus $15,000 in renovations, which translated into a monthly payment of almost $600). However, I chose to pay $750 per month so that I could put the extra $150 towards principal and pay down the loan faster.

Decor and furnishing totaled $30,000. I paid my half out of pocket (thank you Facebook marketplace, Big Lots and garage sales). I spent weeks refinishing old furniture, adding nautical handles to dressers and other little touches to make the home unique. Sweat equity, especially in the beginning years, has always paid me back in cold hard cash. I highly recommend it.

On an ongoing monthly basis, here's how it worked out:

Total In	3,250
Total Out	(1,545)
Net Revenue	1,705

But I still had to pay myself back for the out-of-pocket furniture and decor expense, so my first year cash flow was lower than it would be going forward. The chart on the next page breaks it down.

An added bonus—we purchased in a buyer's market (2015), and it was a foreclosure, so we got the house for cheap.

VACATION RENTAL #2 (50% OWNERSHIP)		
INVESTMENT		
Purchase price	95,000	
Renovations	15,000	
FUNDING		
HELOC	110,000	
REVENUE		39,000
ONGOING EXPENSES		
HELOC Payment	9,000	
Taxes	2,250	
Insurance	2,500	
Utilities & Maintenance	4,800	
Ongoing Annual Expense Total		18,550
ONGOING ANNUAL CASH FLOW		20,450
per month		*1,705*
ONE TIME EXPENSE		
Furniture & Décor	7,500	
FIRST YEAR CASH FLOW		11,050

Years later, around the time we bought out my cousin, the rules in our market had changed, and we were forced to convert the home to a long-term rental. We had managed to pay down our debt tremendously during the years the home was a vacation rental and even managed to pay off our HELOC.

When we bought her out, we did so by taking a mortgage for $120,000 (monthly payment around $1,000).

Today, taxes have gone up, and we now pay $7,000/year ($584/month) in taxes. Fortunately, because we converted the home to a long-term rental, our insurance costs decreased to $3,400/year ($284/month).

Additionally, since the property is no longer a vacation rental we only pay for lawn, pool care and pest control ($250/month) and not all of the utilities.

That home now brings in steady long-term rental income of $3,000 per month, covering its costs and adding profit to my pocket.

Total In	3,000
Total Out	(2,118)
Net Revenue	882

NOW A LONG-TERM RENTAL (100% OWNERSHIP)			
INVESTMENT			
Partner Buyout	120,000		
FUNDING (HELOC)			
Mortgage Amount	120,000		
MONTHLY REVENUE			3,000
MONTHLY EXPENSES			
Mortgage Payment		(1,000)	
Taxes		(584)	
Insurance		(284)	
Maintenance		(250)	
Expense Total:			(2,118)
MONTHLY CASH FLOW			882

Not too shabby.

Here's the kicker. Over the years this home, actually all our homes, have increased in value. This little gem is now worth over $450,000.

Let's unpack that.

We spent $7,500 of our own money to decorate and furnish the home (half of $15,000).

We used a HELOC initially to purchase 50% of the house (meaning, we used the bank's money, not ours).

Over the years, vacation rental guests paid to rent the house, and we paid down our HELOC.

We then took a bank loan years later of $120,000 to buy out my cousin (again, this was the bank's money, not ours).

Through the continued rents, we pay for the pest control, pool maintenance, lawn care, mortgage payment, insurance and taxes. That means someone else (our tenants) are paying for these items, not us.

Since only the $7,500 to decorate came out of our pocket, we can fairly state that we put $7,500 into the house (plus our sweat equity).

Ten years later, our original $7,500 is in a home now valued at $450,000 with a mortgage of less than $100,000 owed.

You may have heard of 10x return on investment my friends but that, Boss Lady, is a **46x** return! ($350,000 equity / $7,500 out-of-pocket investment).

Oh, and Vacation Home #1? The numbers worked out on that one too.

For Vacation Home #1, we put down $50,000. That house is now worth $435,000. More than 8x our initial investment!

That's not the same 46x as house #2. Remember when I said that I should have put more money into renovations on house #1 and less into the down payment? Now you can see why I don't recommend such a big down payment. You make a better return on investment when you use less of your money and let your tenants pay for the house. We'll discuss that a little more later.

Also, it must make sense. Don't read that and think you should go buy a house with as little money down as possible if the house doesn't have a positive cash flow. That would put you owing a ton of money on a home that you may not be able to cover. You make money when you "buy" a home because you will have hopefully made sure the cash flow covers your expenses and reserve.

Vacation Rental 3: The Hard Money Hustle

Next up: a beat-up cottage a stone's throw from the sand, listed at $220,000. This was another "steal" because I was on top of my game watching my market closely. When this house came up for sale, I knew it was listed way under price. Turns out, the then owner had terrible tenants living in the house and just wanted out. That's real estate—prices fluctuate, and if you are paying attention, you will find that you can grab a few properties for deals for all kinds of reasons. Do your research and be ready to act; you will likely reap great rewards.

The house needed a serious facelift: think '80s linoleum floors, crumbling cabinets, and a questionable smell I still can't describe.

I took out a $280,000 hard money loan, gutted the kitchen, added a bedroom and bathroom by enclosing the garage and cutting the living room in half, and turned that toad into a prince. Eight months later, we refinanced the $280,000 we spent ... and the house appraised with a valuation of

$400,000. The hard money loan was repaid entirely from the new mortgage proceeds, leaving me with *zero* of my own cash invested.

Let's review. I used someone else's money to buy and renovate the house. Then, after renovations, I paid all that money back with a bank loan which required no down payment since the appraisal was so high. I then paid that loan back with other people's money (the people renting the house). So, I put zero into that house (except my decorating skills).

Current value today? Over $500,000 and still pulling in bookings every month. And monthly cash flow? Over $1,000 per month.

We are currently installing a pool at that property, using our HELOC to finance it. Once it's ready to go, we will see a huge increase in bookings and our nightly rate will be higher. Thus, increasing our return (again).

Vacation Home 4: Turning Our Farmhouse into a Retreat

Life changes. After several years of investing from afar, we finally left Atlanta for my beloved beach life. That meant we had our sweet A-frame farmhouse in Georgia on seven acres just sitting empty.

Rather than sell it, we listed it as a vacation rental. We were nervous as it's not in a big tourist hotspot—no ocean, no fancy nightlife—but it *is* peaceful, secluded, and stunning in its own rustic way.

We market it for romantic weekends, micro-weddings, girls' weekends, and quiet family holidays. Our two horses that live on the property are an extra hit with guests. Bookings stay steady, covering the mortgage and giving us a little extra income (which we dump back into the mortgage and upgrades to the property). And because the guests love it, we're on track to pay it off three years early.

For this house, we put $100,000 down as we were living in the home when we purchased it and wanted a lower payment. Had we purchased it as an investment only, we would have put down less.

With the vacation rental income, we turned our cash flow for this property from a negative $1,700/month (our mortgage payment) to a positive $400/month. Over nine years, we have a total return of approximately 394% or roughly 43% annualized.

To be fair, it hasn't simply been a set-it-and-forget-it. Over the years we have had "stuff" come up (and at times, literally stuff that came up through the septic system). We've had people try to throw farm parties. We've had to figure out how to have our huge yard maintained and our horses taken care of from a state away.

We've also been able to visit our families that live in Georgia, with our dogs in tow, and stay at *our* home. Not with either of our in-laws. A nice bonus. We get to keep our horses, and they are living their best dream horse life.

Oh, and we are making money, and the house is appreciating.

If you ask me, that's worth dealing with septic tank issues, occasionally demanding guests and a few other issues along the way.

Unleashing Your Inner
🎶 Champion 🎶

Here's a quick snapshot of how the rest of our portfolio came together:

Vacation Rental 5: Conventional mortgage loan, bought below market, light renovation.

Vacation Rental 6: Initially used hard money, renovated, refinanced, rented (the last "R" in BRRRR, repeating the same strategy as Vacation Rental #3)

Vacation Rental 7: Used a Self-directed IRA + two trusted partners. That's retirement money that works double duty.

Vacation Rental 8: Pooled together a small group of investors, used hard money, quick cash-out refi.

Vacation Rental 9: Bought with close friends using a conventional mortgage loan. Earmarked profits for our nieces' and nephews' college funds.

Vacation Rental 10: Mixed-use: our company office is located downstairs, with a vacation rental upstairs. The rental upstairs covers the business rent for our office.

This didn't all happen overnight. It took vision, partners, creativity, and constant learning. As I've said, we are going to go into all these financial strategies (and more) in Chapters 7 and 8. The important part is, I came up with plans and then went into action. Sitting on the sidelines is not for budding Boss Ladies. If you are going to build your empire, you better be ready to start making some moves, even when it gets a little uncomfortable.

There is a reason not everyone plays the real estate game. It can be risky, tricky, hard work and you can even lose money at times. Take a pulse check, momma, and make sure you have skin thick enough to deal with both the ups and the downs.

There will be downs. There will be losses. This is a risk. You must understand that before you decide to play. But oh mama, the upside can be oh-so-sweet!

Think you are ready to do this? If investing in vacation rentals sounds intriguing to you, then keep on reading, sister. Vacation rental is my personal all-time favorite type of real estate investing. You may wonder then, why I don't invest *only* in vacation rentals.

Investing, all types of investing, be it stocks, bonds, mutual funds or real estate, should involve diversification. If I only invested in vacation rentals, I would have myself in a tight spot if the economy took a mega nosedive like we saw in 2007. While I do love them, these types of investments only make sense when the numbers work. It can't ever be "just because I like a house or love a location." Money talks.

Don't Get
♫ *Blown Away* ♫

"Blown Away" makes me think back to the time the hurricane came through town, and the ocean rose higher than it has ever been. One investor friend of mine, whose three direct oceanfront homes my company manages, had two of his properties topple into the ocean. I shit you not. The night before the houses were there, and the next day when we went to check on them for him, they were gone. The news crews came and I'm sure if you Google search you can find the devastation with pictures of my business partner, my dog Dot and me. Talk about a nightmare.

I'm not telling you that to scare you, I'm sharing it with you because it happened.

If you're thinking about how devastated you would be, know this. The man that owns the properties, and his amazing daughter that helps him with all of his investments, never lost their cool. Were they upset? Yes. Devastated and teetering on the edge? Not at all.

How can this be?

They were calm because they had been investing for years and seen all sorts of ups and downs. They had built a portfolio to withstand even the strongest storm. A well-diversified portfolio that protected them when a portion of their investment portfolio was lost.

Not entirely different from the stock market.

Don't worry, they are coming back stronger than ever and ready to continue their investment journey, now with even more gusto.

That comes with learning, hard work, doing, understanding and mitigating risks.

Keep reading, Boss Lady, because you are on the journey to get to that place!

Supercharge Your Maintenance Plan

Remember when we talked about routine maintenance back in Chapter 3? Well, when you step into the world of vacation rentals, you've got to supercharge that preparation. Owning a short-term rental means handling all the same maintenance that comes with a traditional home—plumbing, HVAC, roofing, and appliances—but at a much faster pace and with higher expectations.

Guests expect everything to work perfectly every time they check in. That means if a coffee maker, Wi-Fi router, or washing machine breaks, you can't wait a week to fix it—you need a plan (and a budget) to handle repairs immediately.

On top of that, vacation rentals come with extra upkeep costs that long-term rentals don't. Think upgraded, high-speed Wi-Fi for streaming guests, fresh décor to keep your listings competitive, and periodic furniture replacements from extra wear and tear. You're not just maintaining a property—you're maintaining an experience.

> **ROCKSTAR TIP**
> Keep your property 5-star ready with preventive maintenance, tech upgrades & fresh decor.

Developing Your Portfolio

Pick the Right Market or
♪ Get Out of This Town ♪

Location is everything. For vacation rentals, you want a place that checks most of these boxes:

- Popular destination with year-round draw or a very heavy tourism season that can offset the slow/dead times.
- Not oversaturated with short-term rentals.
- Homes that are reasonably priced, especially when

you compare the cost to what you can earn in nightly rental income.
- Friendly, or at least fair, local short-term rental rules.
- Personal bonus (but not a requirement at all): somewhere you enjoy visiting!

Just because a realtor says a home can be used as a vacation rental property does not mean that it can. Realtors often have no idea what zoning laws exist on vacation rentals. Just this morning, before I began working on this part of the book, I reached out to a realtor that had a property listed as a *"high demand short-term rental investment opportunity."* Because of my extensive background in this field, the address alone was a red flag.

I was heart-broken to find that the agent stood his ground claiming the home was "absolutely allowed to be short-term rented." After explaining to him my credentials and even sending him the tax documents to prove it was not, he still did not believe me.

> **ROCKSTAR TIP**
> Check with the city to confirm the property is zoned for vacation rental before you buy.

This means some poor unsuspecting (and likely newbie) investor will end up buying this property to earn rental income only to find out they are going to be in hot water with the city. The property in question is 100% located in a zone that has a six-month minimum rental requirement, and the city fines owners anywhere from $1,000-$15,000 a day for violations. Don't believe that? Check out Daytona Beach Special Magistrate Hearings online and you will quickly see how many people get snookered on these ... It's truly devastating.

How can you be sure a property is properly zoned? The easiest way is to simply call the city/municipality/county where the property is located and ask. The zoning department will give you the answer. I would recommend asking for an email confirmation as well to CYA.

Don't rely solely on the real estate agent only as many of them don't know what they don't know.

You must crunch your numbers and then crunch them again. Have someone look them over (I have missed things numerous times that my business partner has caught and visa-versa).

Let's run the numbers:

Nightly rate. What's the expected average nightly rate?

Occupancy rate. Be conservative, 50–60% at first. Use Mashvisor or AirDNA to get occupancy rates but keep in mind these services use all properties in the area to get to their numbers, so you need to take your property's specifics into account. Be realistic about the subject property. If you are in a beach town but not actually on the beach, you are going to be lower than the average. On a ski-in/ski-out slope, you may be on the higher side. It's all relative to the comparables.

Expenses. What are all your expenses (mortgage, taxes, insurance, utilities, cleaning, supplies, repairs, platform fees, management)? Don't underestimate; in fact, I try to overestimate expenses by 10% because stuff will always happen.

Then ask: *After ALL of that, do I still make money?*

> **ROCKSTAR TIP**
> Research occupancy and average daily rates on AirDNA or Mashvisor before you buy.

My bar for short-term rentals is a bit higher than for long-term rentals because of the additional costs associated with them. For short-term rentals I need to know that I will make 1.5% of the purchase price in monthly rental income ... in a lower interest rate market that number might even move to 2%.

That means, if I buy a house for $250,000 (all in with costs of furniture and décor), I better be making at least $3,750/month in income to make it a good vacation rental.

Rental revenue is the key here. You must pay attention that you are calculating JUST the rental revenue. Vacation rentals bring in money for cleaning fees, damage waivers, taxes and more, but those fees typically get paid out to someone else (for example, the cleaners get paid to clean). Sites like Airbnb, VRBO and Booking.com charge anywhere from 8-15% to use their site.

Your calculations need to be based on the rental revenue that you will receive for the nightly rental rate, not the gross revenue that includes all the other fees.

If the answer isn't a strong YES, walk away. A bad deal you *force* will drain you faster than a cheap margarita hangover.

Financing — Be a Creative ♫ Cowgirl Casanov-ette ♫

You already know the drill by now, I am going to go into how to pay for your real estate investments in Chapters 7 and 8, but it's worth a note here that these are the most common ways I see vacation rental homes funded:

- Cash (great if you've got it, but rare for newbies)
- Conventional loan (best rates, usually 10–20% down)
- Second home loan (requires you to use it yourself part of the year)
- HELOC (tap equity in another property)
- Hard money (high-interest, short-term loan—best for flips/renos)
- Partnerships (share the costs and profits)

Mix and match. Get creative. Just be clear with partners: spell out who does what, who gets paid what, and who calls the shots.

Design to Dazzle
🎶 *Temporary Home* 🎶

Average homes sit empty. Beautiful, photo-worthy homes book up fast and command higher nightly rates.

Design is your superpower:

- Pick a theme that fits the location (coastal, boho, modern rustic)
- Use bold, fun colors-no bland beige!
- Add local art or quirky touches guests will photograph.
- Invest in comfy mattresses, soft linens, quality towels.
- Think Instagrammable moments: a swing chair, a mural, a neon sign.

Think about when you book a vacation home (or daydream about them while scrolling through Instagram). What stands out to you?

Dot com rental sites often have hundreds to thousands of listings in some areas. If you want to get your place rented, you need to stand out.

We own a property management company with a portfolio of over a hundred properties. At this point, we won't accept a new property into our portfolio if it doesn't have some "special" component. Think outside of the box on this. Some examples at our properties are pool tables, game rooms, crazy kids-themed rooms, awesome outdoor spaces, cowboy pools, oceanfront, golf carts that come with your rental, mini-golf course in the backyard. The possibilities are endless.

In the modern vacation era, a basic house with little to no amenities, boring décor and no "sparkle" needs to be sent to your long-term rental portfolio. Vacation rentals require extras. Just like basic hotels (think Motel 6) don't have high occupancy and charge low rates, the same is true for vacation rentals. If you don't make yours special, you are just a low-end motel waiting to fail.

Once you have your vacation space set up and ready to go, hire a professional photographer. Worth every penny.

Get Legit Legally so You Don't ♬ Undo It ♬

We already went over this, but I am going to say it again as missing this has cost many an investor their entire retirement plan. Check local laws *before* you buy. Many cities limit short-term rentals, require permits, or enforce zoning rules. Ignore this and you risk huge fines or a forced shutdown.

Get proper insurance. Short-term rental insurance is different from homeowner's insurance. You don't want to find out you have the wrong insurance after someone falls down the steps, or worse. Make sure to fully disclose to your insurance agent what you are doing, then make sure your policy covers it. Short-term rental insurance is more costly than residential homeowners, as it should be. You are a lot more likely to get sued by someone staying at the house for a week than by your spouse or child falling down the stairs.

Have a rock-solid rental agreement and clear house rules.

Set up your tax structure. Talk to a CPA about LLCs and tax deductions. There can be huge tax benefits available to you when investing in real estate. Learn them, use them and make sure your tax person has a strong knowledge.

Do I Need an LLC?

When we first started investing, my husband and I were pretty clueless. When we purchased our first investment home, we put the deed in our *personal* names. It wasn't until the next deal that we knew to put the property in an LLC.

I get asked all the time, should I put my investment properties in an LLC? Likely, but check with an attorney as all situations are different.

While legal advice is extremely valuable, not everyone starts off with their property in an LLC. Nope, sorry rule followers. I'm not going to pretend that everyone does, which isn't to say that everyone should or shouldn't. I've just been in this game a long time, and I know a whole lotta people that didn't or never have put properties in an LLC. I didn't at first, so I'm not going to mislead you. But if you are worried about your liability (and you should be), an attorney is well worth what you will pay. It only takes one lawsuit for you to realize how expensive not having your properties set up correctly can be. If you put the property in your own name or in a partnership, make sure you clearly understand the risks involved.

Many years ago, an ex-friend of mine, (who also happened to *be* an attorney), was (unbeknownst to me) drowning in debt. Turns out, just because someone is an attorney does not mean they understand money. This crazy lady stole her (now ex) husband's credit and racked up thousands of dollars in debt. Once she ran through his assets and credit, she was desperate for money and decided to sue me because she knew I had assets (don't worry, I kicked her ass in court). Karma always wins, and she eventually lost her job at a major law firm and had to move across the country to escape her own chaos.

But still, I had been sued, which cost a small fortune to defend even if it was a petty lawsuit *and* even though she lost. I have found there are lessons in almost everything in life, and this was no exception. At the time, I lived in Georgia, where my primary residence could have been in jeopardy had the lawsuit gone the wrong way.

Live and learn. After the drama and heartache of that experience, we hired an asset protection attorney and now have a structure so that we can protect our assets. But that *also* came at a high cost. We would have saved ourselves a lot of hassle had we set things up correctly at the front-end.

If you are going to be serious about real estate investing, and you want to fully protect yourself, you should talk to an attorney.

For those of you that have very few assets, you are probably less likely to have someone do a "money grab" on you than those of you that have a lot to lose. But if you are reading this book and thinking about investing in real estate, I truly hope that means you have some assets. Remember, poor people don't get sued; rich people do. Act accordingly.

Memorable Experiences
The ♫ Good in Goodbye ♫

How do you make your listing shine? Here are some tips:

Title and Description. Write a title and description that spark curiosity. Again, creativity is key here. My bestie and I own several rentals together. We name them all after 90's rap themes such as: Beach Gangsta's Paradise or 99 Problems but the Beach Ain't One. We even use gangsta slang in our listing description. Sounds silly, right? Wrong. Our units outperform the market because they are fun. People like renting from people that seem fun.

Photography. Use high-quality, well-lit photos. Do not skimp here. Hire a photographer and if you are near something cool, pay for the drone footage. Update photos as you update things at your property.

Welcome pets. I will argue with you all day long that the benefits of allowing pets (dogs in particular) at your rentals will more than outweigh almost any real or perceived negative. I allow dogs at all my units. Guests pay extra for pets which helps cover the extra cleaning and puts extra dough in your pocket. I have yet to see any rental anywhere that the costs associated with allowing dogs outweighed the cons. Pet lovers travel with their pets. They also usually take good care of their pups, so these animals are typically reasonably well trained.

Amenities. List all amenities, people love details! Add small ticket items that people need but don't want to travel with—blow dryers, irons, toiletries.

Responsiveness. Respond fast to inquiries. Can't be available quickly? Hire a property manager.

Thoughtful touches. Treat guests like royalty: leave welcome baskets, local guides, snacks, or handwritten notes.

Happy guests = five-star reviews = higher rankings = more bookings. It's a beautiful cycle.

Automate and Delegate
♬ *Jesus Take The Wheel* ♬

Yes, you *can* manage it yourself at first. I did. But eventually, your time is more valuable spent finding your next deal than scrubbing toilets. Who should you hire:

- A local cleaner (pay well, they're your MVP)
- A handyman for emergencies
- A co-host or property manager if you travel a lot or have conflicts that would make you unreachable for guests. The last thing you want is a 1-star review because you were at work while a guest was sweating it out in July with no A/C.

Use tech. We implement as much technology in our vacation rentals as possible. It saves you money in the long run, but more importantly, it saves you aggravation. When a guest can't figure out how to turn down the A/C and it's a hundred degrees in Florida, there is nothing like saying, "Hold on while I do that for you on my app." Here are tech items we use for our homes:

- Smart locks
- Smart thermostats/pool timers/alarms
- Welcome screens
- Automated messages
- Calendar sync across platforms
- Dynamic pricing software
- Software to schedule your cleaners if you are self-managing.

Some things can't or shouldn't be automated. You want your guests to feel special and not like just another guest. Take the time to ask your guests questions like, "Are you celebrating anything on your trip"? If they are, leave a balloon that says, "Happy Anniversary" or a note with "Good luck on your Cheerleading Competition!" Small gestures go a long way.

Work smarter, not harder.

How to Level Up: Advanced Play for ♫ Good Girls ♫

Once you have a couple of successful properties, it's time to up your game. Here are some ways to level up:

Create a direct booking website. Save on platform fees. You make more on direct bookings.

Build an email list. Invite past guests back with discounts.

Offer add-ons. Think private chefs, beach equipment rentals, or adventure packages.

Host special events. Small weddings, retreats, photoshoots.

These extra income streams separate the average hosts from the pro hosts.

One of my goals with this book is to help you get to your dreams a little faster than I did, and that means telling you about a few tools and strategies I wish someone had told *me* about years ago.

Let's start with Property Management Software (PMS systems).

Whether you're managing short-term or long-term rentals, there are dozens of software options available to help you streamline your operations. These tools can automate bookings, guest communication, maintenance schedules, owner statements, task assignments, you name it. If you've got more than a couple of properties, you need to start shopping for software. There are also platforms specifically for maintenance, cleaning, and project coordination. Because your portfolio will look different than mine, you'll need to find the system that fits your business best. I'll include a list of recommended tools and resources at the end of this book.

Another game-changer? Conferences.

There are local, national, and even international conferences for rental property owners, both short-term and long-term. Go to one. Seriously. Attend a reputable event, walk the vendor hall, sit in the sessions, and talk to other investors. You will learn more in two days than you could in six months of Googling. It's an investment in your knowledge and your network, and it's one of the best moves I've ever made.

If you're in the vacation rental space, let's talk about damage waivers.

No more collecting security deposits. All they do is set you up for awkward conversations when something goes wrong. We once had a guest break a brand-new twin bed on its *first night of use*. Was it a pillow fight? A little too much "vacation romance"? A larger guest? Who knows, and honestly, who wants to have that conversation? If I called that guest to tell them I was keeping their deposit, I'd be hit with a one-star review, guaranteed. A damage waiver solves all that. It's a small fee guests pay (you can even make a little profit from it), and it protects them from being charged directly for accidental damage. You simply file a claim, fix or replace the item, and move on. No drama. That's what five-star service looks like.

Offer or require trip insurance. Especially for coastal properties during hurricane season, it's a must. If a guest needs to cancel, or worse, if you must evacuate them mid-stay due to weather, you won't be stuck arguing about refunds. With trip insurance, they're covered, you're covered, and you still get paid. That's a win-win.

Avoid My Mistakes

Learn from my face plants so you don't repeat them.

Things I Wish I'd Known Sooner
♬ Lessons Learned ♬

Don't underestimate start-up costs. Budget 15–20% more than you think.

Don't ignore local laws. Trust me, fighting city hall is not fun.

Don't skimp on cleaners. A bad review about cleanliness kills bookings fast.

Don't pick cheap furniture. It breaks. Buy sturdy.

Don't rely on one platform. List on multiple sites to fill your calendar.

It's Not Passive
♬ The Fighter ♬

Here's the raw truth: Vacation rentals are not "set it and forget it". Even with property managers, things go wrong. Guests break stuff. Hurricanes happen. Furnishings wear out. Zoning changes. Competition increases.

But if you love real estate, design, and creating magical stays for strangers? It's the most fun way I know to build wealth.

This business turned me from a woman scraping rock bottom into a woman who built ten vacation homes, financial freedom, and a brand that pays for adventures and family memories.

And the best part? You can start TODAY.

Vacation rentals can be wildly profitable, but they're also tied closely to economic conditions, tourism trends, and even headline news. When the economy is booming, people book getaways like it's their job. But when a downturn hits? Travel plans are often the first thing to get slashed.

We all lived through COVID: the travel bans, the cancellations, the uncertainty. Many vacation rental owners saw their calendars go from fully booked to completely empty in a matter of days. Cities with riots or civil unrest have seen similar impacts. When safety becomes a concern, even the dreamiest beachfront listing can sit vacant. And guess what? Those mortgage payments don't disappear just because guests do.

Then there are the unicorn moments, like the Taylor Swift Eras Tour. In some cities, hosts were pulling in numbers they'd never seen before (and probably won't see again anytime soon). Don't build your projections off a one-time tour stop or a viral event. That's not your baseline, that's a bonus.

The lesson? Always plan for the ups *and* the downs. Have reserves. Protect yourself with guest insurance to cover flexible cancellation policies (most of the sites reward hosts with flexible cancellation policies with higher rankings so even though I don't love them, I do offer pretty flexible cancel policies), diversified revenue strategies, and, if possible, business insurance for income loss. Vacation rentals are still one of my favorite investment vehicles, but it's not all sunshine and five-star reviews.

Smart Boss Ladies know to prepare for the storm *before* it hits, literally and financially.

Buy the Beach House
🎶 *Crazy Dreams* 🎶

Boss Lady, don't wait for perfection. Don't wait for a huge savings account or the "perfect time." I started broken and bruised, and I turned my heartbreak into beachfront dreams.

You can too.

Do your research. Run the numbers. Build your plan. Then trust yourself enough to take that first step.

Because one day, I promise, you'll be standing barefoot on your own deck, coffee in hand, salty breeze on your face, smiling at the version of yourself who dared to do it scared.

Now go. *Buy the damn beach house!*

Chapter 5
FIX-AND-FLIPS

♫ *Just Give Me a Reason* ♫

Alright, let's spill some tea.

If long-term rentals are the steady boyfriend who's good to you year after year, fix-and-flip investing is that wild fling that keeps you up at night, but done right, drops serious cash in your bank account.

Flipping houses is real estate's rock concert.

It's messy, fast, high-reward, and sometimes full of drama, but oh, Boss Lady, when you get it right, there is *nothing* like turning a sad, run-down house into a beautiful, profitable masterpiece.

Think of fix-and-flips as your Prada or Louis—bold, high-stakes, and not for the faint of heart.

How Flips Work

🎶 Just Like Fire 🎶

A successful flip depends on one simple idea: Buy LOW, Fix Smart, Sell HIGH.

This means: Buy under market value. **The money is made when you buy.**

One of the most important truths in real estate, whether you're flipping, buying a rental, or investing in a vacation property, is this: the money is made at the purchase.

Not during the sale. Not during the renovation. **The moment you buy.**

> **MIC DROP MOMENT**
>
> In real estate, the money is made at the purchase. Buy smart, or don't buy at all.

If you're not getting a great deal on the front end, it's going to be extremely difficult, sometimes impossible, to make a real profit. Flipping is all about margins. If you're buying at or near retail value, there's no room for error, and let me tell you, errors *will* happen. Renovations run over budget. Timelines get delayed. The market shifts. And suddenly, that thin profit margin is gone, and you're left holding the bag (and this time it's that expensive Prada or Louis).

The same goes for other types of real estate investing, too. Even with rentals, if you overpay for the property or fail to factor in all your expenses (like repairs, vacancies, taxes, or property management), your cash flow disappears before it even begins. It doesn't matter how trendy the area is or how cute the kitchen turns out, if the numbers don't work on day one, they're probably not going to magically work later. With flips, the problem is even more intense because you don't have time to make up for errors.

Be relentless in your evaluation. Run the numbers. Ask the hard questions. Be willing to walk away.

Because in real estate, profit isn't luck, it's strategy. And the first move in that strategy is always this: buy smart, or don't buy at all.

Why Flipping Works *and* Is Fun

What makes flipping such a great investment strategy?

- Big, fast cash injections—way more up-front profit than holding rentals.
- Opportunity to flex your creativity—design, stage, and shine.
- Recycle your capital—flip profits can fund long-term rentals or other flips.
- Opportunity to learn construction, negotiating, and project management.

But a word of truth: It's not HGTV. You won't magically paint a wall and double your money overnight.

You need clear math, plenty of grit, a sharp eye for detail and a Plan B for when things go sideways.

Understand Flips so You Don't Have ♬ Trouble ♬

If you're going to get into flipping (or even rehabbing a rental) you need to go in with your eyes wide open when it comes to repair and renovation costs. The reality is this: construction estimates are almost always under budget, not because contractors are out to get you (although sometimes they are), but because there are *so many unknowns* until the work begins.

Ever heard the phrase *"opening Pandora's box?"* That's exactly what happens when you take down a wall. What looks like a simple layout change might suddenly reveal old wiring, termite damage, mold, rotten framing, or unpermitted plumbing. And once you open it, you can't ignore it, you *have* to fix it.

On top of that, the price of materials is constantly fluctuating. Lumber, appliances, tile, paint—these can all jump in cost seemingly overnight. What looked like a $40,000 rehab could easily turn into a $60,000 one and, if you didn't pad your budget, that can leave you in a bad situation. That's why I always tell new investors: budget for what you *know*, then add 10-20% for what you don't.

If you're new to construction or flipping, it's a smart move to partner with someone more experienced for your first project. The right partner can help you avoid costly mistakes and save you from hiring the wrong people. Speaking of which ...

Let's talk a little more about contractors.

Yes, some are fantastic: reliable, honest, and skilled. But there are also plenty of horror stories. I've seen contractors take a deposit and disappear. I've seen work half-finished, inspections failed, and crews that vanish the moment a payment clears. Don't think it won't happen to you? This is a reality of the business, and the best way to protect yourself is to follow standard industry payment structures:

- 1/3 up-front (after signing a detailed contract)
- 1/3 at midpoint (when agreed-upon milestones are met)
- 1/3 upon completion and approval of work

Never, and I mean *never*, pay 100% up-front. And don't be afraid to ask for photos, references, and a copy of their license and insurance.

Real estate is a business, and construction is one of its most expensive (and risky) components. If you treat it casually, you'll pay for it, literally. But if you budget wisely, hire smart, and plan for the unexpected, you'll be the one sympathizing with others' horror stories, not telling your own.

Nail Your Renovation Budget
♫ U + UR Hand♫-yman

This is where rookies lose money. Every time.

Common rookie mistake: budgeting what you *hope* repairs cost instead of getting actual quotes.

Here are the smart moves a Boss Lady makes:

- Walk the property with a contractor *before* you buy.
- Get line item estimates.
- Add a 10–20% contingency for surprises. (Trust me, there are *always* surprises.)
- Focus on improvements that raise value: kitchens, bathrooms, curb appeal.
- Know your area. Avoid custom luxury upgrades that buyers won't pay extra for in a mid-tier neighborhood.

- Start in areas that are low- to middle-grade; don't attempt your first flip on a luxury golf course lot. Get your feet wet on smaller projects, then scale up.

If you're flipping or rehabbing a property, your renovation budget can make or break your deal, literally. That's why it's critical to nail your numbers before the first hammer swings.

Start by getting clear, detailed bids in writing from your contractors. Don't settle for vague estimates like "around $10,000 for everything". You need line-by-line breakdowns: labor, materials, permits, timelines, so you know exactly what's included and what's not. Does the bid include trash haul-away? Who's responsible for purchasing materials? Are appliances included, or is that on you? Misunderstandings here can cost you thousands.

Also, take a hard look at what you can realistically do yourself. When I was getting started, I had more time than money, so I painted many of my first project houses myself. Did I want to hire someone? Yes. Did it save me money? Also, yes. These days, I have contractors do it because my time is more valuable elsewhere, but back then, DIY made a huge difference. If you're handy and willing to get your hands dirty, you can stretch your budget by taking on smaller tasks like painting, landscaping, or demo.

Now, let's talk about surprises because there *will* be some.

No matter how well you plan, renovation almost always costs more than you expect. You open a wall and find outdated wiring. The plumbing isn't up to code. Material prices spike. That "just needs paint" bathroom turns into a full gut job. This is normal and why I keep recommending adding a cushion of 10–20% on top of your renovation budget for the unexpected.

Planning ahead doesn't eliminate surprises, but it protects your profits from hurdles. Because in real estate, the ones who succeed aren't the ones who never hit a bump in the road, they're the ones who budgeted for the potholes.

The Money Side of Flips

The 70% Rule: Almost
*♫ F*kin Perfect ♫*

A classic investor rule of thumb is the 70% Rule.

Let's look at an example.

You are considering purchasing a home in a decent neighborhood. Similar homes that are in excellent shape sell for $300,000. We'll use $300,000 as the After Repair Value (ARV). You estimate $40,000 in repairs to get yours up to snuff. What should you pay for this property?

70% of ARV ($300,000) = $210,000
$210,000 - $40,000 repairs = $170,000

Don't pay more than $170,000 for this flip.

THE 70% RULE

Max Purchase Price =
(ARV * 70%)
minus Repair Costs

Why not? Because your renovation estimates could be off (when you find things behind the walls that you didn't expect or for a myriad of other unforeseen repairs). Plus, the cushion covers closing costs, realtor commissions, holding costs—and your profit.

Finance Your Flip

🎶 Get the Party Started 🎶

Cash is Queen. But let's be real; not everyone has a mountain of Benjamins lying around. And even if you do, using all your cash on one flip may not be the smartest move when you could leverage financing and keep multiple projects rolling at the same time. Boss Ladies know money makes more money, but only if you put it to work.

Here are some common ways to fund your flip:

Cash. Clean, fast, and simple. Sellers love cash offers because they often close quickly and without financing headaches. You'll avoid interest payments and loan fees, which means more profit in your pocket.

The downside? Tying up all your funds in one project can limit how many deals you can do at once.

As you learned in the previous chapters, there are ways to pay "cash" without actually having to save up for years.

Hard Money and DSCR Loans. We've briefly touched on hard money loans. DSCR loans are short-term, high-interest loans designed specifically for investors. They're asset-based, meaning the lender cares more about the property's value and ARV (After Repair Value) than your personal credit.

Both are perfect for flips if used wisely: they give you quick access to capital, but you've got to finish fast because interest rates can be steep.

Private Money. This usually comes from friends, family, or local investors who want a return but aren't traditional lenders. Terms can be flexible and negotiated to fit your deal (interest-only payments, balloon payments, etc.).

The key here is trust—protect those relationships with solid contracts and clear expectations.

Partnerships. Teamwork makes the dream work! You bring the hustle (finding, managing, and flipping the property) while your partner brings the cash. Profits are split, but this strategy lets you take on bigger projects and share the risk.

Just like with private money, always put partnership terms in writing to avoid messy "he said, she said" situations later.

We'll be getting into the nitty-gritty of these (and other) funding strategies later in Chapters 7 and 8. But for now, know this: you don't have to have a bank account bursting with cash to start flipping. You just need the right mix of strategy, confidence, and Boss Lady resourcefulness.

♬ Who Knew ♬
More Than ♬ Stupid Girls ♬

Our gender, in general, tends to overthink. If you don't, rock on sister! You are a role model for us all.

But if you are like us other 99%, overthinking is another one of our superpowers.

Showing care and taking pride in what we do are also our superpowers, though, and combined in the right portions, can be the perfect formula for a delicious real estate recipe.

Don't be scared of making mistakes—men do it every day without losing a wink of sleep. Your job isn't to be perfect; it's to learn, adjust, and keep moving forward. Princesses don't waste time on nonsense—we're in training to become queens. Learn the lesson, take the win, and move on with your crown still intact.

P!nk said it best: "Girls with ambition—that's what I want to see."

And she's right. Ambition is not something to apologize for; it's something to celebrate.

So please, don't let fear be the thing that holds you back. Try. Risk. Dream. Take the first step even if your knees are shaking. Every queen you admire started exactly where you are—one brave choice at a time.

Let's look at a worst-case scenario.

What if I invest all of my money into something and lose it all?

That's the fear, right?

The answer is easy .... *don't invest it all!* Start with smaller properties, spread out your risk and invest with groups of people that *you know and trust, and be sure to have all your legal ducks in a row with them.* Set a financial goal that would get you in position to feel comfortable investing in real estate. Perhaps a goal using one of the financial strategies you learned in *"Becoming a Boss Lady Investor."*

I didn't do my first flip until I was ready. Until I was educated enough to feel comfortable and confident. I read numerous books on the topic, listened to podcasts and talked to other investors. You will know when you are ready. That's one of the beautiful parts of being a woman—you have women's intuition. Trust that, it's usually right. Use your head for the numbers, but your heart to guide your progress.

Find Your Flip

Know Your Market Like
♫ Nobody Knows ♫

Flippers fail when they *guess* what buyers want.

Your renovation must match what *actual buyers* in that neighborhood expect—no more, no less.

How do you find out what buyers want? You do your research like a boss:

- Walk open houses. See finishes, layouts, and colors that sell.
- Chat up local realtors. They know what's hot and can tell you about the market trends.
- Check "days on market" for recent flips. Quick sales mean the flipper nailed it; slow means overpriced or over-renovated.
- Study the comps (comparable sales), not just listings. List prices lie; sale prices tell the truth.

Find a Killer Flip
♫ Try ♫

Good flips don't fall in your lap. You hustle for them. Where do you look?

Multiple Listing Service. Many flips come from standard listings overlooked by regular buyers.

Off-market Properties. Send letters to absentee owners, tired landlords, or distressed sellers.

Wholesalers. Build relationships, they find deals and assign them to you for a fee.

Auctions and Foreclosure Sales. Riskier, but sometimes goldmines.

Drive for Dollars. Spot ugly houses in good areas. Look for overgrown yards, peeling paint, neglected roofs, signs the owner may be open to sell.

If you're serious about flipping houses, let me be real with you: it might take a while to find a good one. I don't just casually scroll Zillow once a month and magically stumble upon profit-packed properties, and neither do most successful investors. I look almost *every single day*. So do the other investors. If you only give a fraction of yourself, don't expect a full-on victory.

Finding a profitable flip takes effort and consistency. It means putting your name out there, building your network, talking to wholesalers, checking online platforms regularly, and sending letters to homeowners in foreclosure, people with tax liens, absentee owners, and estates. But most importantly, it means building genuine relationships, because those are what ultimately lead to opportunities.

Deals don't just fall in your lap.

Until they do.

Last year, I did two flips that literally landed in my lap, but they only happened because I'd done the work beforehand.

Here's how one of them went down.

A woman from one of my networking groups (read between the lines, get out there and network) reached out to me about a financial situation involving her son. He was facing foreclosure, and she wanted to help him avoid that if possible. Since she knew I was in real estate investing from our networking, she reached out to me and asked if I would be willing to help. I want to stress how impactful networking can be. Yes, it can be intimidating. Yes, you will walk into rooms where you may not know anybody. But, yes, it can help you build your portfolio. It works because you end up building meaningful relationships if you are authentic. My networking-made friend reached out because we had built a relationship and she *trusted me*. That trust opened the door.

I met with her and her son. He was $50,000 behind on his mortgage with no foreseeable way out. I offered a solution: I'd bring the mortgage current on payments and help him to avoid foreclosure. In exchange, he would add me to the deed and vacate the home within thirty days. Then, after I renovated and sold the house, he would get 10% of the net profit. It was a win-win. Without me, he would be stuck with ten years of wrecked credit and nothing to show for it. With me, he avoided foreclosure, started rebuilding his credit, and walked away with cash to restart his life.

I then brought in my bestie and business partner not just because we love working together, but because she has access to private funding. I found the deal and had the contractor; she brought the money. Her private lender, someone we'd worked with before, funded the deal in less than a week.

We made the mortgage current, did some light renovations, and sold the home just four months after the initial meeting. My partner and I each pocketed $30,000. Total time I spent on the deal? Maybe twenty hours.

That's $1,500 an hour.

Not bad for a deal built on trust, preparation, connections and maybe a little wine and laughter.

But let me tell you, they're not all that easy.

Just a few months later, my bestie investing partner and I had a similar situation brought to us, this time involving a property in Virginia with a nightmare tenant issue. This one was *way* more of a headache. We had to hire an attorney, navigate a painfully slow eviction process (Virginia is *very* tenant-friendly), and manage a much more serious renovation. Did I mention that neither of us lives in Virginia?

It took us almost a year to get the tenant out, fix the property, and finally get it sold. But here's the key: we had budgeted for the unexpected, done our homework, and had solid numbers going in. We knew the potential, and we were prepared for the mess.

In the end, we each walked away with $25,000. Not quite as juicy as the first deal, but not too shabby for about fifty hours of work, which may even be an overestimation. That's still $500 an hour, and more importantly, a massive learning experience that we'll use to make the next deal even smoother. You can see why earlier I shared that a five-dollar cup of coffee could be almost offensive. My time is valuable. Because I have put in tremendous amounts of time, money and energy to learn all the things.

Bottom line? Not every flip will be easy. Not every deal will be fun. But if you're consistent, well-connected, and prepared, the right opportunities *will* come, and when they do, you'll be ready to turn them into profit.

Don't Fall in Love with the Flip

Listen closely, Boss Lady, this part is important: You *cannot* get emotionally attached to a flip. It's not your dream home. It's not your forever kitchen. It's not the tile you'd pick for yourself. It's a product, and you're in the business of selling it for profit.

> **ROCKSTAR TIP**
>
> Don't fall in love with the *property*. Fall in love with the *deal*.

The worst mistake you can make at this stage? Letting your ego, emotions, or pride dictate your price.

I get it. You put in time, effort, and energy. You picked finishes, oversaw contractors, maybe even cleaned up drywall dust yourself. But once that property is ready to sell, you've got to take a deep breath and treat it like what it is: an asset, not a passion project.

And here's the truth: The market will tell you if your price is fair.

If you're priced right, you'll get calls, showings, and offers. If you're priced too high, crickets. On the flip side (no pun intended), if you price it way below market value and it still sits? Something's off. Maybe the layout is awkward. Maybe your renovations were not up to par. Maybe it just doesn't "feel" right to buyers. Don't ignore that, adjust.

The goal here isn't to win a pricing war. It's to close this chapter and move on to the next profitable deal. The time you waste obsessing over one flip could be time spent analyzing the next opportunity, building your portfolio, or let's be real, just enjoying the fruits of your labor.

Detach. Sell smart. Move on.

That's how you build real momentum, and real wealth, in this game.

Renovations

Assemble Your Rock Band
♫ *Please Don't Leave Me* ♫

Flipping is a team sport. No one does it alone, and you don't want to! Your flip dream team should include:

- Real estate agent who knows flips & ARV
- General contractor (GC) with a proven track record
- Inspector who spots hidden problems
- Title company familiar with investment deals
- Hard money, business partners or private lender
- Accountant to handle tax implications
- A great photographer that knows how to capture your flip perfectly to make it stand out in the crowd.

Vet everyone. One bad contractor or flaky lender can kill a deal faster than you can say "dry rot."

Having the right team will be the difference between those that succeed and those that don't.

Renovate with Purpose
♫ *There You Go* ♫

When it comes to flipping a house, renovate with intention … *and* emotion. That's right, use your female superpowers to guide you in making your flip a project you are proud to put on the market. While this isn't the time to design your dream home or get carried away with high-end finishes, adding a few special touches to make your home a nice place for its future owner isn't a crime (and can even positively impact your bottom line). Don't be afraid to add some pizazz or uniqueness. I'm a fan of making your home nicer, perhaps even more environmentally friendly, than the last owner. I firmly believe it's our job as humans to leave things nicer than we found them.

That being said, you also cannot dismiss that your goal is profit, not Pinterest perfection. Choose wisely, use your special "woman's touch" and leave your sparkle. Just make sure there is enough *financial* sparkle that it makes sense.

I realize you can make more money by cutting corners, and there will likely be places along the way that you will need to. That's okay. But as you can, when you can, do the best you can. Don't lose your soul along the way, sister. That's what makes you special!

In a vacation rental, I might go all out—install a pool, add a game room, or invest in quirky, Instagrammable décor that creates a standout guest experience. But with a flip? The strategy is completely different. Your job is to make the property slightly nicer than the average home in the area, not so luxurious that you price yourself out of the neighborhood, but just enough that it stands out to buyers, sells quickly and provides the next owner a safe, quality home.

This means understanding your comps (comparable sales). Find out what similar homes in the area are selling for. What features do they have? What finishes are considered standard, what are upgrades? What could you do to make your flip stand out? What could you add to make yours more modern, while still considering heritage features?

What I have found with women investors is that we get worried about and second guess our decisions. Shocking, I know.

Girl, sometimes you just have to go for it. Make your decision and then carry forward. You'll make mistakes; you'll learn along the way. I'll say it again. *Done is better than perfect.*

That's not to say over-renovating isn't a real risk. You may think adding crown molding or top-of-the-line appliances will impress buyers, but if those upgrades don't translate to a higher sales price, you're cutting into your profit margin. On the flip side, cutting too many corners or skipping key updates can leave the home sitting on the market, and every day it doesn't sell is money out of your pocket.

Give the house broad appeal. Make it clean, safe, fresh, and move-in ready. Stick to neutral colors, modern fixtures, and functional layouts. Think *desirable, but affordable*. And always remember you're not keeping this home, you're selling it. Make every renovation decision with your future buyer in mind.

High-Impact Renovations
♬ *Walk Me Home* ♬

When it comes to flipping houses, not all renovations are created equal. If you're working with a limited budget (and let's be honest, most of us are), you've got to be strategic about where you spend your money. Focus on the improvements that actually add value, not just the ones that make the house look cute or feel cozy.

So where should you invest?

Kitchens and Bathrooms Sell Homes. Always. Buyers will forgive a lot of other flaws if the kitchen and bathrooms feel clean, modern, and updated. You don't need to go overboard with designer finishes, but replacing dated cabinets, adding new countertops (quartz or granite if the neighborhood justifies it), installing a backsplash, and upgrading fixtures can give you a huge return. In bathrooms, focus on the master bath first; it's one of the most emotionally driven spaces for buyers. New vanities, tile, and modern fixtures go a long way.

New Fixtures Make a Big Difference. Light fixtures, door hardware, faucets—these are small upgrades that instantly modernize a space and make it feel more high-end. They're also relatively inexpensive but deliver a high perceived value.

Flooring and Paint = Instant Refresh. Fresh, neutral paint and consistent, durable flooring throughout the home are non-negotiable in most flips. They're basic, yes, but powerful. Think light, bright, and move-in ready.

What *Not* to Spend Big On. Fences, elaborate landscaping, specialty upgrades (like built-in shelving, high-end wine fridges, or hot tubs) usually don't provide a great return unless you're in an upscale area (which we've already discussed is not where to get started in flipping). These features may feel like nice touches, but they rarely sway a buyer's decision, and they almost never increase the appraised value enough to justify the cost.

Rule of Thumb: If the improvement won't help sell the house faster or raise the appraised value, don't do it. In a flip, you're not building your forever home; you're building someone else's "good enough" home that looks great and sells fast.

Prioritize improvements that buyers can see, feel, and appreciate, especially in the areas that sell houses: kitchens, bathrooms, and the overall vibe. Everything else? Only if the budget allows.

Manage Like a CEO
♫ *All I Know So Far* ♫

This is where Boss Ladies always shine. Project management is our secret weapon.

You're the Captain, so steer the ship.

Don't fall into the trap of thinking that once the renovation starts, your job is done. Wrong. If you're flipping a house, you're the project manager, the boss, the one at the helm. And if you're not steering, don't be surprised when things go off course—over budget, behind schedule, or completely sideways.

Remember these golden rules of flipping:

- Have a written scope of work: room by room, detail by detail.
- Sign a contract with your General Contractor (GC). Include deadlines, payment stages, and penalties for delays.
- Keep a paper trail. Get receipts. Put all changes to the contract (scope, cost, timeline, materials) in writing.
- Visit the site regularly, or have someone you trust that can. Pictures aren't enough.
- Pay your contractor in draws, not all up-front!

Even when I'm not physically at the property, I'm still managing the renovation every step of the way. When we flipped the house in Virginia, we didn't just hand it over and hope for the best. We had a plan.

I stayed in constant communication with our contractor, checking in regularly, asking for photo updates, and making sure milestones were met on time. I even had a local locksmith who agreed to keep me posted on tenant activity before the eviction. I paid him a little something on the side, totally worth it for the peace of mind and extra eyes on the property.

My bestie scheduled a visit to see her boyfriend (he lives a few hours from the property) and made a stopover to check on the house mid-renovation. That in-person visit helped us verify progress, reinforce accountability, and spot a couple of minor issues before they turned into big ones.

Bonus, her flight was a write off.

Our contractor? He was a referral from our realtor. Our realtor was a referral from a business partner in one of our other ventures. That's how deep our networking and relationship-building runs. You never know who knows your next key player, but when you treat people well, follow through, and stay professional, those connections pay off in big ways.

Timelines, budgets, communication: they're everything. Even if you're not swinging a hammer, your role is critical. Check progress. Ask questions. Get photos. Review receipts. Create a simple spreadsheet and track what's happening and when. Be present, even if you're remote.

You are the captain of this renovation. Run the ship like you mean it because no one else is going to care about your investment like you do.

Remember: Time is money. Every extra day accumulates expense: carrying costs, loan interest, taxes, insurance.

Sell Smart, Sell Fast

🎶 *Raise Your Glass* 🎶

You made the house beautiful, now maximize your payday. Here are some tips for getting your flip sold fast:

Price realistically. Check sold comps, not wishful thinking.

Stage the home. Empty houses feel cold—a little furniture works magic.

Hire a professional photographer. Cell phone pics are not good enough and will cost you thousands.

Launch with a bang. List your property on Thursday, have an open house on the weekend, create urgency.

Be confident but flexible in negotiations. Don't get greedy and lose a good buyer.

One of the most common mistakes I see new female flippers make is getting emotionally attached to a sales number. I get it. You put your time, energy, and money into the property, and you believe it is worth top dollar, maybe even a little more. But here's the scoop: your flip is only worth what someone is willing to pay for it *today.* Don't get so stuck on a number that you can't see the forest through the trees. Markets go up *and* down.

Sites like Zillow have provided tremendous value in many areas. But one area I think we are seeing it hurt people is in price adjustments. Two years ago, my main market was H.O.T. hot. You could list a house for over market price and have five offers in less than a week. Zillow adjusted its data to reflect that. The problem is, many of us were checking the prices of our own homes to see the value, make us feel richer, or just out of curiosity. No matter the reason, we saw our homes priced at those high numbers and became attached to those numbers.

That same market has declined significantly in the last couple of years. We have way fewer buyers than sellers. Homes are sitting on the market for extended periods of time. Yet sellers refuse to lower their prices. I think that is the psychological damage of *seeing* a potential value for our homes and creating that false wealth in our heads. We don't have that money until we sell and, nowadays, the number in my market tends to be less. That's a hard pill for many to swallow. But it is a reality.

Every market is different. Some markets were declining while my main market was rapidly increasing and vice versa.

Markets go up *and* down. Never forget that.

I have seen investors with crazy returns in a super-charged market suddenly become penniless in a downturn because they sat on properties too long or weren't prepared to have to hold on for a while.

Real estate markets will always go up *and* down. In my lifetime, there have been four big "up" markets and three broad "down" markets. Real estate market upturns and downtowns have existed since people started buying and selling real estate. That is what a *market* is, so don't let that scare you, just let that guide you in your decision making.

When flipping, your goal is simple: get in, renovate smart, and sell fast.

Holding out for an extra $10,000 might *feel* like a smart move, but if it takes you significantly longer to sell, you could easily lose that profit (and more) in carrying costs, not to mention the opportunity cost of having your money tied up in a property that's just sitting there.

Here's an example. Let's say your flip has a monthly mortgage and expense total of $3,000. If you decide to hold out three extra months hoping for a $10,000 higher sale price, that delay costs you $9,000 in carrying expenses—and that's before factoring in lost time you could've spent working on your *next* profitable project.

Boss Lady Translation: You didn't make an extra $10,000—you lost time, cash flow, and momentum.

> **MIC DROP MOMENT**
> In the world of fix-and-flip, speed is part of your profit strategy.

Every day your flip sits on the market, your profits shrink. Price it right from the start. Understand that shooting for the stars may work, but if it doesn't, react accordingly and in a timely fashion. Time is of the essence.

Make sure when you are researching *recent* comps you are not just looking at "For Sale" listings, but *actual closed sales.* Be honest with yourself about how your property stacks up. Is it slightly nicer? Great. Price it just above the comp. Does the comp down the street have granite counters and an updated bathroom but you don't? Price accordingly. Are you in an area that would justify large shifts, like a tourist town or a rapidly growing hotspot, or is the growth in your area steady? Find a balance between best price, time on market and profit.

The smartest flippers aren't the ones who make the biggest score—they're the ones who understand when to let go of the number in their head and focus on the number in their pocket. Don't let your pride cost you your profit. Sell smart. Sell fast. Move on to the next opportunity.

And on the occasion that you don't make what you thought or worse, lose money, don't beat yourself up. It happens to everyone at some point. However, if it's happening to you more often than you are making money, then you need to do a self-evaluation. What can you change in your formula to make it work?

Flippin' Good Advice

♬ Who Knew ♬

Let's keep it real: Flipping can bite you if you're careless.

I don't know if you have ever been to a P!nk concert, but watching her acrobatically twirl while suspended mid-air is breathtaking. To be able to do this, she trains, trains and trains again. She does this so that when it matters most, she doesn't make a mistake. I want you to do the same, Boss Lady.

Fix-and-Flip Pitfalls to Avoid

♬ Just Like a Pill ♬

Let's review some of the most common mistakes I see when newbies are flipping homes.

- Overpaying because you fell in love with the house
- Underestimating repairs
- Adding upgrades buyers won't pay extra for
- Not checking for hidden issues (foundation, mold, pests)
- Hiring cheap, bad contractors
- Not having a clear exit plan—know the goal of how long you want to hold the property and what your plans are with the money once you sell.
- Holding too long and letting carrying costs eat profit

Be Ready to Pivot

Sometimes a house looks like a flip but ends up making more sense as a rental. If you find yourself in a scenario that has you thinking it might be time to flip your flip into a rental, ask yourself:

Is the neighborhood appreciating fast? FLIP IT. When home values are rising quickly, you can often sell now, capture that equity gain immediately, and roll your profits into the next deal before the market shifts.

Is it in a stable area with high rental demand? Maybe KEEP IT. If rents are strong and vacancies are low, holding the property can provide steady cash flow and long-term appreciation, only if the numbers work.

Does it need only cosmetic work? FLIP IT. Cosmetic flips (paint, flooring, fixtures) mean lower renovation costs and faster turnaround-perfect for a quick, profitable resale.

Does it have strong cash flow potential? RENT IT. If the property can consistently cover its expenses and generate monthly income, that's wealth you can hold and grow over time.

Long-term, the most wealth often comes from *owning*, not just flipping. Many flippers end up holding their best deals and renting them out.

Be ready to pivot. I've turned flips into long-term rentals and vacation rentals. I've turned vacation rentals into long-term rentals. I've turned long-terms into flips. The market, the property and your current personal situation can change, and you need to be prepared to pivot.

Advanced Flip Tactics for Serious Boss Ladies

Ready to play bigger? Here are a few more strategies to consider:

Wholesaling. Buy a distressed house, clean it up minimally, resell fast without full reno.

Live-in Flip. Buy a fixer as your primary home, renovate while living there, sell after 2 years, pay ZERO capital gains up to $250k ($500k married). Legal tax cheat code!

BRRRR to Flip. Combine the BRRRR (Buy, Rehab, Rent, Refi, Repeat) method with a flip. Hold if the market dips; sell when it's hot.

Flip Like a Boss Lady
♬ *A Million Dreams* ♬

Get out your pen and paper. Create a checklist or use mine. There are always deals to be had; you just have to believe in yourself and get started.

- Clarify your target area, visit open houses weekly.
- Build your team: agent, lender, contractor, inspector.
- Secure financing approval before you shop.
- Analyze multiple deals. Make low offers until one sticks.
- Walk the property with your GC before closing.
- Lock your scope, timeline, and payment draws.
- Visit the site at least 2–3 times a week.
- List smart, stage, price right, sell fast.

Flipping isn't a hobby. It is a business. Treat it like one, and it will fund your freedom.

Be patient. Be disciplined. Run your numbers ruthlessly. Trust your gut *and* your calculator.

One day you'll look back and see how that single flip changed your confidence, your bank balance, and your whole life trajectory.

I believe in you—now go make that ugly duckling a swan and cash that check.

You are a Boss Lady Investor.

This is your power move.

Now flip it and watch your bottom line climb.

Chapter 6
MULTI-FAMILY PROPERTIES

♫ *Run the World (Girls)* ♫

Boss Lady, refill that coffee (or pour another bold glass of wine, no judgment) because we're diving into one of the most impactful, yet misunderstood, ways to grow your wealth in real estate: multi-family unit investing.

When I was a kid, one of my favorite games was Monopoly. Even though it felt like my siblings always seemed to win, I was fascinated by the strategy of gathering properties then adding houses and eventually hotels. Little did I realize that the lessons Monopoly was teaching were more applicable to real life than most of the algebraic equations I would be taught years later in high school.

Let's do a little review first. As you have already learned, single-family residential properties are without a doubt the most common and often the easiest way to dip your toes into the investing pool. One tenant, one roof, one yard to mow. It's straightforward, often easier to finance than other types of investments, and doesn't require quite the same learning curve as more complex strategies. For many investors (me included), that's exactly where the journey starts.

But eventually, as your confidence (and bank account) grows, you may start looking for what's next. That's where multi-family unit investing comes in. Think duplexes, triplexes, four-plexes or even your first small apartment building.

The benefits? They're real and they're powerful. Multiple income streams under one roof means one insurance policy, one mortgage, and more opportunities to offset vacancies. If one tenant moves out, you still have rent rolling in from the others. Your expenses don't rise as fast as your income potential does. That's why multi-family investing can feel like strapping a turbo engine onto your wealth-building strategy.

But it's not without its challenges, and I want to be clear about that.

Here's a personal story. I once bought a multi-unit complex that I was super excited about. We had just finished renovating the entire building—I'm talking fresh everything. Then a hurricane hit (I live and invest quite a bit in Florida, so hurricanes are one of our consistent risks). The roof was ripped off, water poured in, and the entire building was uninhabitable. Suddenly, I had no rental income, massive carrying costs, and a huge insurance deductible. Everything inside was water damaged. It was a gut punch.

So yes, while multi-family investing has a ton of potential, it also comes with risk, especially when you're starting out. The learning curve can be steep. Repairs are bigger. Property management can be more intense. And the stakes are higher when multiple tenants are relying on you.

This chapter is meant to give you the foundational knowledge—enough tools in your kit so that if a great deal does come across your desk, you don't have to walk away simply because you didn't understand the basics. And maybe, just maybe, multi-family becomes your passion. Maybe it's to you what vacation rentals are to me—the thing you love, the thing that lights you up.

If that's the case? Lean in. Follow your heart (so long as the numbers make investment sense). This might not be your first step, but it could be the one that makes your heart flutter and your bank account soar.

The Basics

Let's break it down so there's zero confusion because real estate jargon can sound more complicated than it is. Multi-family simply means more than one housing unit on a single parcel. There are two core types of multi-family properties: residential and commercial.

Residential (or Small) Multi-family Units. These are properties with 2-4 rental units. These properties offer a huge perk: they qualify for conventional residential loans. This means lower interest rates, longer terms, and easier approvals than big commercial loans. These are especially great (if you can find them) for investors that want to live on the property and rent out the other units to offset, and even cover, their mortgage.

Commercial Multi-family Units. These are properties with 5 or more rental units. Now you're in *commercial* territory. The bank doesn't care as much about your personal income; instead, they care about the building's income. If the building makes money, you're golden.

Let's not make this sound too simple though. You will likely need to work with a lender that believes in you for these types of properties. If you have little to no track record, it can be extremely difficult to find financing. Your personal credit will probably be tied to the note with a personal guarantee—that means you are on the hook no matter what, so you better have exceptional credit with strong rent rolls.

The good news is these types of loans often won't "show" on your personal credit as long as you don't default. Why is this cool? Because then you can use your credit to buy more investments! When you're further along in the journey, this will get easier and, at some point, you may not even need to have your personal credit tied to the investment ... but that's a long way down the road.

Remember way back in Chapter 3 when I said single-family homes are like your classic, go-to purse, your Coach bag—practical, reliable, and easy to pair with anything? Multi-family investing? That's your Goyard or high-end travel trunk: spacious, valuable, and made to carry a serious load while taking you places.

With one purchase, you get multiple income streams. You're building wealth and hedging risk all in one move. It's chess, not checkers and you're the queen.

From One House to an Empire

Before they were building empires, many of today's top real estate investors, especially women blazing trails in a male-dominated space, were buying one home at a time. Don't let social media fool you. Most investors didn't start with a 100-unit apartment complex or a luxury development. They started with a single-family rental ... just like the one you might be eyeing right now.

Take powerhouse investor Barbara Corcoran, who launched her real estate career with a $1,000 loan and a tiny apartment in New York. Or Elisa Zhang, who began with a townhome and eventually scaled to over 1,000 units through smart multi-family moves. And let's not forget Kathy Fettke, who began with a single-family property and now helps thousands of investors grow wealth through residential and commercial real estate.

Think of it like playing *Monopoly*. You don't win by going straight to Boardwalk and Park Place and building hotels. You start by buying the little green houses on Baltic Avenue. You collect rent. You learn the game. And eventually, *when the time is right*, you trade up for the red hotels. That's how wealth is built: house by house, move by move.

There's no shame in starting small. In fact, it's where the smartest players begin. Single-family homes teach you the fundamentals: tenant screening, budgeting for repairs, building equity, understanding market cycles. In my opinion, once you master that game, then you're ready for the next level.

If you're looking at a simple little rental house thinking, "Is this enough?" The answer is YES. It's more than enough. It's your first green house on the path to hotel-level wealth.

Now, let's get you ready to grow with some benefits of multi-family investing.

Benefits of Owning ♫ Sandcastles ♫

Let's unpack why this strategy is so beloved by seasoned investors. There are plenty of reasons these have become the darlings of many real estate investors.

Economies of Scale. One roof. One yard. One insurance policy. One property tax bill. But *four* rent checks. You do the math.

For example, four single-family homes scattered across a city mean four roofs to maintain, four lawns to mow, four pest control appointments, four insurance policies. A fourplex means ONE of each, but four streams of income. Your per-unit cost drops dramatically, which supercharges your cash flow.

I'm going to walk you through the numbers on that in just a moment. Hang tight.

Lower Risk. Single-family rentals are great until they're vacant—then you're on the hook for 100% of the mortgage out of pocket.

With a fourplex? If one unit goes empty, you're still 75% occupied and collecting rent to cover expenses. It's called risk mitigation, and it's the backbone of a stress-resistant portfolio.

Streamlined Management. Hiring a property manager? It's far cheaper and more efficient to pay them to manage four units in one building than four houses scattered across town. And if you are self-managing or just checking in, it's more efficient for you, too. Less driving, fewer contractors to coordinate, fewer headaches.

Flexible Financing Options. Best-kept secret: a 2–4 unit property keeps you in residential loan territory. This means that when buying a multi-unit with four or fewer units you can still qualify for:

- FHA loans (only 3.5% down!)
- VA loans (zero down if you qualify)
- Conventional loans (typically 15–25% down)

Above four units? Yes, you will have to use a commercial loan, but that's not a bad thing either! Commercial financing means your approval is based on the *income potential* of the property. That means your personal salary doesn't have to do all the heavy lifting.

Forced Appreciation. Single-family homes mostly appreciate when the neighborhood improves, or the market lifts all boats. Multi-family properties can appreciate because *you* boost their income.

Raise rents a little? Cut expenses with better utilities or self-managing lawn care? Boom: the property is worth more. Why? Because the building's value is tied directly to its income. How so?

With income properties, the value of your building isn't based on what you ***paid*** for it or how cute the paint color is, it's based on how much money it puts in your pocket every year.

That number is called Net Operating Income (NOI). Investors and appraisers use NOI and the market's Cap Rate (read on, I'll cover Cap Rate shortly) to figure out what a property earning that much cash is worth.

I heard that sigh. I know. I just threw some scary technical terms at you. But don't worry. I'm going to go through this step by step. Before you know it, you'll be bantering these terms around like you've known them your whole life.

Math You Actually Need

Let's be real—knowing the Pythagorean Theorem has never helped me get out of debt, buy a rental property, or build a retirement plan. I still can't tell a hypotenuse from a hippopotamus, but I *can* tell you how to make your money work for you.

Net Operating Income (NOI)

Net Operating Income is all the rent you collect minus the day-to-day expenses like taxes, insurance, utilities you cover, lawn care, and repairs. Mortgage payments don't count here.

NET OPERATING INCOME

REVENUE - EXPENSES (EXCEPT MORTGAGE PAYMENTS)

Gross Rent Multiplier (GRM)

Gross Rent Multiplier is a handy way to screen potential deals. It quickly separates the wheat from the chaff, so to speak.

GROSS RENT MULTIPLIER

PURCHASE PRICE / ANNUAL GROSS RENT

The *lower* the GRM, the better the cash flow potential. Seems backwards, I know, but it makes sense.

A good target GRM is between 4 to 8, depending on the market.

Let's look at an example for a fourplex:

GROSS RENT MULTIPLIER, EXAMPLE 1	
INVESTMENT	
Purchase price	800,000
MONTHLY REVENUE	
4 units @ $1,700/unit	6,800
ANNUAL REVENUE	
*Monthy Revenue * 12*	81,600
GRM	
$800,00 / $81,600	9.8

A GRM near 10 is a red flag. It means the property might not cash flow well—especially after you factor in insurance, taxes, repairs, management, and vacancies. At best, you're looking at slim margins. At worst, you're paying to own it.

Here's another example for a fourplex with better rent:

GROSS RENT MULTIPLER, EXAMPLE 2	
INVESTMENT	
Purchase price	800,000
MONTHLY REVENUE	
4 units @ $2,500/unit	10,000
ANNUAL REVENUE	
*Monthy Revenue * 12*	120,000
GRM	
$800,00 / $81,600	6.7

A GRM under 7 is much more attractive; it's a sign there may be real cash flow potential. But GRM alone doesn't tell you the full story (or account for expenses). So, let's take it a step further ... Enter Cap Rate: The Real MVP of Deal Analysis

Capitalization Rate

Cap Rate, short for Capitalization Rate, tells you how much profit you're making compared to what you paid for the property. Think of it like your return on investment before loans or mortgage payments come into play. It is expressed as a percentage.

$$\text{Cap Rate} = (\text{NOI} \div \text{Purchase Price}) \times 100$$

You already know what NOI is. Just divide NOI by the purchase price, then multiply by 100. Easy peasy. Let's use that second example above and do a Cap Rate calculation.

CAPITALIZATION RATE	
INVESTMENT	
Purchase price	800,000
MONTHLY REVENUE	
4 units @ $2,500/unit	10,000
ANNUAL REVENUE	
*Monthy Revenue * 12*	120,000
GRM	6.7
ANNUAL EXPENSES	
Taxes, Insurance, Maintenance	27,800.0
NET OPERATING INCOME (NOI)	
Annual Revenue - Annual Expenses	92,200
CAP RATE	11.5%

The *higher* the Cap Rate, the better the deal because it's more income for the same investment.

Some Cap Rate norms (these can change with the economy and location, but are a good rule of thumb):

- 4–5%: Common in ultra-competitive or high-end areas (but low cash flow!)
- 6–7%: Solid in many markets, just make sure the property is in great shape.
- 8–10%+: Ding ding ding! You're likely looking at strong cash flow.

So, the 11.5% in our example, *now that's a deal worth chasing!*

Just to keep things clear:

GRM (Gross Rent Multiplier) is your quick screening tool.

- Lower numbers = better cash flow potential
- Think of GRM as the *speed date* of deal analysis

Cap Rate is the more serious deep dive.

- Higher numbers = stronger income
- This is your *second date with spreadsheets and real numbers*

Cap Rate doesn't account for your mortgage or financing, but it *does* help you compare properties quickly and objectively. Want to invest like a pro? Know your Cap Rate and aim for one that reflects your financial goals and risk tolerance.

Don't let the excitement of a multi-family deal cloud your judgment. Use GRM as a quick screen. Use Cap Rate for deeper insight. And above all, use numbers that are conservative and accurate—not what a listing agent *thinks* you can

ROCKSTAR TIP

Use GRM as a quick screen. Use Cap Rate for deeper insight.

charge or what Zillow *dreams* it's worth.

When in doubt? Walk away. If it doesn't have good cash flow, it doesn't go in your portfolio. Period.

Market Value

Remember when I said earlier that investors and appraisers look at the market's Cap Rate to figure out what a property is worth? Now you have the numbers to do this. The formula they use is simple:

MARKET VALUE = NOI ÷ CAP RATE.

Now here's the fun part, the part where "forced appreciation" becomes a reality.

If you nudge income up or trim expenses down, your NOI rises, and because value is tied directly to that number, the property's price tag jumps. It's that simple.

Picture this:

Your four-unit building brings in $5,000 a month in rent, or $60,000 a year. After expenses, you're left with $35,000 in NOI. If similar buildings in your market trade at a 7% Cap Rate, the math says your property is worth around $500,000.

What if you raise rents just $25 per unit per month (totally reasonable with a small value-add like fresh paint or new hardware) and decide to self-manage the lawn to save a few bucks? That tiny rent bump adds about $1,200 a year. Cutting lawn care saves another $800.

New NOI: $37,000.

At the same 7% Cap Rate, the value jumps to roughly **$528,000.**

That's almost *thirty thousand dollars* of equity created from a few small, very doable moves.

The higher value also opens other doors:

> **Refinance power.** With a bigger appraised value and stronger income, you can pull cash out to fund your next deal.
>
> **Selling strength.** Buyers pay for income. A higher NOI means a higher sale price, period.

Boss Lady Takeaway: You don't always need a dramatic renovation to create serious wealth. Sometimes the most powerful upgrades are the quiet ones: a modest rent increase paired with smart expense cuts. Think of it as polishing your crown: subtle, strategic, and completely in your control.

♫ *Deja Vu* ♫

Back in Chapter 3, I talked about the 1% Rule. It is a common benchmark used by real estate investors to quickly evaluate the potential cash flow of single-family rental properties. Here's a quick refresher:

For example, a purchase price of $250,000 should bring in at least $2,500 monthly rent. If it passes that rule, it's worth further analysis for potential cash flow.

> **THE 1% RULE**
>
> A rental income at least 1% of the purchase price will likely have positive cash flow.

Don't forget, the 1% Rule fluctuates. As I write this book, 0.6-0.8% is the norm. When I wrote *Becoming a Boss Lady Investor,* over 1.5% was closer to the norm. Markets, all markets, fluctuate. Mortgage rates, interest rates, insurance and even acceptable investment return numbers all fluctuate.

But you get the drift, the 1% Rule is simple to understand and doesn't really involve much math.

But when it comes to fourplexes or multi-family properties, the approach shifts. You *can* apply the 1% Rule to multi-family properties as a quick filter, but most savvy investors instead focus on more precise metrics (i.e. there is going to be a *little more* math involved).

Cash Flow and Cash-on-Cash Return

We talked about cash flow in both Chapters 3 & 4 because cash flow is a key component of most types of real estate investing. Multi-family investing is no different—if the money coming in doesn't cover the money going out, you're paying for your investment (i.e., you're losing money).

If the cash flow covers your expenses (including setting aside "buckets" for future issues) and puts some dough in your pocket, you're making money.

It's that simple. Make this one of the key points you take from this book.

What's the Difference Between Cash Flow and Cash-on-Cash Return?

Cash flow is the actual dollars left in your pocket each month (or year) after all expenses are paid.

Cash-on-cash return (CoC) tells you the percentage return on the actual cash you invested in the deal. It's a performance metric used to evaluate how hard your money is working for you.

$$\text{Cash-on-Cash Return} = (\text{Annual Cash Flow} \div \text{Cash Invested}) \times 100$$

Your cash invested typically includes the down payment, closing costs, and initial repairs; but for simplicity, we'll only use down payment here.

What's a "Good" Cash-on-Cash Return?

There's no one-size-fits-all answer, but many investors aim for a CoC return of 8–12% on multi-family properties (and even for long-term and short-term rentals).

For comparison, the average stock market return over time is around 7–8% annually. So, if your rental property earns 10–12% cash-on-cash, you're already beating Wall Street, and doing it with an asset you can improve, control, and leverage.

CAP RATE and CASH-ON-CASH RETURN	
INVESTMENT	
Purchase price	800,000
Down Payment	160,000
MONTHLY REVENUE	
4 units @ $2,500 /unit	10,000
ANNUAL REVENUE	
Monthly Revenue * 12	120,000
GRM	
Purchase price / Annual Gross Rent	6.7
ANNUAL REVENUE	
Monthly Revenue * 12	120,000
ANNUAL EXPENSES	
Mortgage	49,812
Taxes, Insurance, Maintenance	27,800
CASH FLOW (NOI)	
Annual Revenue - Annual Expenses	42,388
CAP RATE	
(NOI / Purchase Price) *100	5.3%
CASH-ON-CASH RETURN	
Cash Flow / Cash Invested	26.5%

Let's say you buy a rental property with a down payment of $30,000 and an annual cash flow (after all expenses and mortgage payments) of $3,600. The cash-on-cash return is $30,000 (the down payment) divided by $3,600 (the annual cash flow) which equals 0.12, or 12%, better than the average return you'd get from most index funds or stocks.

Real estate gives you something the stock market doesn't—control. You can increase rents, reduce expenses, add amenities, or refinance to boost your returns. In this game, *you're the CEO of your own investment portfolio.*

You can also use these formulas for long-term and short-term rental investing.

I promise, we are almost done with the math portion. But let's get you prepared for what the lenders may be looking for when you go to buy your first multi-family.

Occupancy and Vacancy

There are a couple of other numbers you will want to be familiar with as you look at multi-family unit investments.

Staying Full
♬ *All Night* ♬

Occupancy Rate

This the percentage of rentable units that are currently occupied by paying tenants, expressed as a percentage. It answers the question: *"How full is this property?"*

OCCUPANCY RATE =
OCCUPIED UNITS / TOTAL UNITS

Let's look at an example. You're analyzing a 4-unit property. 3 units are currently rented, and 1 is vacant. The Occupancy Rate is 3 divided by 4, or 75%

Occupancy rate demonstrates how much of your potential income you're collecting. The building is 75% occupied, meaning you're only collecting 75% of its rent potential. It affects your cash flow, NOI, and property value. Lenders often require a minimum occupancy rate for financing (usually 90%+).

Vacancy Rate

Vacancy is the opposite of occupancy.

VACANCY RATE = 100% - OCCUPANCY RATE

In the example above, the Vacancy Rate is 100% minus 75% (the occupancy rate) which is 25%. Vacancy equals lost income. That's why it matters.

When analyzing deals, always account for less than 100% occupancy, even if the current tenants are solid. A 5-10% vacancy reserve in your numbers keeps your projections realistic and protects your bottom line.

But how will you know what the occupancy rate will be when you are first looking at an investment?

Ask the seller or property manager. Always cross-check the seller's records with bank statements or tax filings when possible. If the numbers on paper don't match the story being told, that's your cue to dig deeper

Review Current Rent Rolls. A rent roll is basically a spreadsheet or report that lists each unit, its current tenant, the lease term, and the monthly rent amount. You can request this directly from the seller, property manager, or listing agent as part of your due diligence. Look for:

- Which units are leased and for how much
- When leases expire (to see if turnover is coming soon)
- Any vacant units or below-market rents that could be raised later

Compare the current rents on the rent roll to market rent data (using tools like Zillow, Apartments.com, or Rentometer) to see if there's upside potential or if the property's already maxed out.

> **ROCKSTAR TIP**
> Compare the current rent roll to market data to identify upside potential.

Look at Historical Records. Historical financials show how the property has actually performed over time. Ask for profit-and-loss (P&L) statements, income and expense reports, or tax returns for the past 12–24 months. These will show patterns in:

- Rent collected vs. vacancies
- Maintenance and repair costs
- Utilities, property management fees, and insurance
- Any irregular expenses that could affect future profits

Call a *local* property management company. They will know the typical occupancy in the area.

Always confirm how many total rentable units the property has. Perhaps the property is listed as an eightplex, but one of the units is really only used for storage because it has no windows and is too small to meet the city's minimum square footage requirements. The total rentable units here would be 7, not 8.

What If the property is vacant or underperforming?

Don't panic, this could mean opportunity. Maybe the property needs a face lift. Maybe the current owners bought it in 1954, and it still has pink bathtubs. You'll have to figure that out to see if opportunity exists. Use Google or AI to find the average multi-family occupancy rate for an area. If you do need to renovate, calculate if some or all of the units will be unavailable during that time.

If the average market occupancy is 92%, use 90% to be safe. Always leave room for unexpected vacancies.

Effective Gross Income

Now that you have a realistic occupancy rate, it's time to refine your financials. Instead of looking at the (unlikely) income from 100% full occupancy, we're going to use Effective Gross Income. To find this number, multiply the total potential rent (if all units were full) by your expected occupancy rate.

Effective Gross Income =
Potential Gross Income × Occupancy Rate

Here is an example using a 90% occupancy rate.

POTENTIAL vs EFFECTIVE GROSS INCOME	
100% Occupancy	
*4 units @ $2,500/unit * 12 months*	
POTENTIAL GROSS INCOME	120,000
Occupancy Rate @ 90%	
EFFECTIVE GROSS INCOME	108,000

The Effective Gross Income is the real number you plug into your NOI calculation, not the full $120,000, unless you're *absolutely sure* you'll be 100% full all the time (spoiler: you won't). This will change your Cap Rate and your Cash-on-Cash Return. Let's do this using our earlier example.

CAP RATE and CASH-ON-CASH RETURN	POTENTIAL	EFFECTIVE
Purchase price	800,000	800,000
Down Payment	160,000	160,000
ANNUAL REVENUE		
*Monthly Revenue * 12*	120,000	108000
Occupancy	100%	90%
ANNUAL EXPENSES		
Mortgage	49,812	49,812
Taxes, Insurance, Maintenance	27,800	27,800
CASH FLOW (NOI)		
Annual Revenue - Annual Expens	42,388	30,388
CAP RATE		
*(NOI / Purchase Price) *100*	5.3%	3.8%
CASH-ON-CASH RETURN		
Cash Flow / Cash Invested	26.5%	19.0%

The new, more realistic Cap Rate is 3.8% (not 5.3%), and the new, more realistic Cash-on-Cash Return is 19% (not 26.5%).

Once we replace the unrealistic 100% occupancy projection with a real occupancy rate, the property's annual income goes down, and that alone reduces the Cap Rate from 5.3% to 3.8% and the Cash-on-Cash Return from 26.5% to 19%. Same property, same expenses, just more honest math. Check with investor forums like Bigger Pockets or reach out to real estate investor-friendly agents in your area to determine what a good "current" cap rate is for your area (as cap rates, like most investment markets, shift with the times).

Beware: 100% occupancy is not always a shining green light; if the current rent is below market, it could be a giant red flag. It means something is off ... maybe there are hidden problems with the building, or the location is undesirable. Something is forcing the lower rents, and you need to find out what that is.

> **ROCKSTAR TIP**
> Don't favor occupancy over cash flow. If occupancy is 100%, make sure the rent is at market rate.

Final Thought: Occupancy tells you how much money is actually hitting your bank account, not just what *could* come in. Run your numbers based on realistic expectations, and you'll avoid getting stuck with a pretty building that's secretly draining your wallet.

> **BACKSTAGE PASS**
> Leverage is a power tool to build wealth fast. But it most be used wisely.

You don't have to crunch every number by hand—there are fantastic online tools and calculators that make analyzing deals a breeze. Platforms like BiggerPockets, Roofstock, and DealCheck can help you estimate cash flow, cap rates, and returns using real data. Plug in your purchase price, projected rent, and expenses, and you'll instantly see if a property's worth your time, or if you should keep looking for a better deal.

Find It and Own It

The Hunt

♫ *If I Were a Boy* ♫

How do you find the "perfect" multi-family property investment?

Breaking news: you don't need to know a secret handshake or come from old money. Finding good multi-family properties to invest in will likely take more work than finding single-family homes but remember - you are a lioness! Here's how Boss

Ladies find killer deals. You're going to recognize a lot of these from previous chapters.

MLS Listings/Zillow. Yes, good multi-families hide in plain sight. Work with an agent who understands the nuances of investment properties (one that doesn't try to talk you into spending more than investment numbers justify).

Off-Market Deals. Build a network of wholesalers, contractors, and real estate agents. Tell *everyone* you're buying. Deals find you.

Local REIAs. Real Estate Investor Associations are networking goldmines. People gossip, trade deals, and share tips. Be there.

Driving for Dollars. See a tired duplex with overgrown grass? Drop a note or knock on the door.

Online Platforms. LoopNet, Crexi, BiggerPockets, Facebook Marketplace — filter by multi-family and set alerts.

Remember: Great deals are MADE, not found. Creative offers, smart negotiation, and vision separate average investors from Boss Ladies.

Rookie Mistakes

🎶 *Naughty Girl* 🎶

I love you too much to let you trip over the obvious. Here are classic traps to avoid.

Overestimating Rent. Use real rental comps not your daydream number. Ask local property managers for realistic ranges. Compare those numbers to what the agent tells you.

The agent will often represent numbers given to her by the sellers. I can't tell you the significant number of times this information has been misleading or plain false. If it's not in line with similar properties nearby, or if it sounds too good to be true ... you know the deal.

Ignoring Hidden Costs. Taxes, insurance, repairs, pest control, vacancy—budget them all. Surprise expenses kill cash flow. Use the same lessons from before. Make sure to use YOUR tax and insurance numbers, NOT what the previous owner paid.

Weak Tenant Screening. Bad tenants cost more than no tenants. Screen thoroughly, run background checks, verify income.

Falling in Love Emotionally. We've been here before Boss Lady. As you already know, women tend to make better investors than men. We also tend to fall in love more quickly than men. Know the difference between a quickie (like a walk-through of a pretty complex that doesn't make financial sense) and a long-term relationship (an investment that makes sense and serves all your needs).

Analysis Paralysis. Some deals are good enough—perfection is a myth. Run the math, trust the process, take action.

Real Talk: ♬ Drunk in Love ♬

Truth bomb: multi-family isn't a crockpot strategy; you can't just set it and walk away. More units mean:

- More toilets break.
- More people can fight.
- More rent checks to chase if you don't screen well.

- Commercial properties have different requirements for construction.
- Commercial properties (think apartment complexes over 4 units) usually require signage, licenses and other additional expenses.

But here's the upside: the *rewards* scale too. Higher cash flow, faster equity gains, and one day, you wake up with income streams that cover your lifestyle.

Boss Ladies don't avoid challenges; we plan for them, budget for them, and keep moving.

Now let's talk about how we finance them.

Chapter 7
TRADITIONAL FINANCING

♬ *Rain on Me* ♬

This is the chapter where it all comes together. You understand the investment options of long-term rentals, short-term vacation rentals, fix-and-flips and multi-family unit investing. You're ready to buy some real estate and start building your empire. You've done the vision board, you've walked a few properties, maybe even stalked Zillow listings like it's your full-time job. But now comes the question that stops way too many would-be investors in their (stiletto-clad) tracks:

"How the heck am I supposed to afford this?"

I promised you way back in Chapter 2 that we would cover funding. Let's get into that now, starting with the ways you've probably already been thinking about. You'll find a summary of all these options in the Appendix.

Cash

Cash is queen. When it comes to real estate, cash really does rule the kingdom. When you make an all-cash offer on a property, assuming other variables (like price) are the same, it puts you ahead of almost every other offer. Cash can open doors and close deals faster than almost any other type of payment.

Keep Your 🎶 *Poker Face* 🎶

I met my husband playing poker. When he entered the room, I was royally flushed, he was *so handsome*. But I couldn't start acting like a schoolgirl, becoming giddy and revealing how immediately gaga I was over him. No, instead, I played it cool, kept a straight face and got to know him during the game. In doing so, I was able to read him better than he thought and not only did I take all his money that night (and he would argue that I have been doing so ever since lol), but I ended up keeping him, too.

You need the same strategy when you are offering cash on a deal. Don't show all your cards. Cash will typically give you the best opportunity to pay the least for a property so don't start jumping up and down when you walk into the perfect property. Play it cool girl, negotiate, whittle down the purchase price and it will pay you back in spades.

The Royal Perks of Cash
🎶 *Perfect Illusion* 🎶

At the end of a real estate transaction, whether you use $300,000 cash or get a $300,000 mortgage to buy the house, the seller still walks away with $300,000 (minus closing fees). So why is cash so beloved?

Sellers love cash because there's no lender to slow things down or deny financing at the last minute. When you make an offer using any type of financing, there is usually a financing contingency that accompanies your offer. This means you only have to buy the house if the lender agrees to the financing. If the lender walks away, the contract is over, and the seller will likely have to start over. With cash, there is no lender and no financing contingency. So, you can see why your offer often jumps to the top of the pile, sometimes even if it's a little lower than a financed bid.

Some other perks of buying with cash:

Speedy Closings. No mortgage underwriting means you can close in days instead of weeks. That speed can score you discounts or win hot properties in competitive markets.

No Interest or Loan Fees. Every dollar you *don't* pay in interest, origination fees, or mortgage insurance is money that stays in your pocket. This can be a lot of money over time. For example, on a $300,000, 30-year conventional mortgage at 6% interest, you will pay $647,514 over the life of the loan. That means you are paying interest to a bank of $347,515. You end up paying more than the original loan amount in interest alone, if you stick with the standard schedule and never refinance or make extra payments. Not the case with cash.

Peace of Mind. No monthly mortgage payment means more flexibility and less stress if rents dip or a unit sits vacant. If you have a few months with no tenant, it's a lot less stressful if you are not having to pay a mortgage payment while you have no rent coming in.

Cash is sounding pretty good right? Not so fast. To every ying there is a yang.

There are hidden downsides to cash purchases:

Tied-up capital. Once you drop that cash, it's locked in the property. Unless you refinance later, you can't use it for other deals or emergencies.

Opportunity cost. Cash in one property might mean missing out on two or three other investments where financing could let you multiply your returns.

Smart Leverage. Real estate wealth is often built by using other people's money. A 10% gain on a fully-cashed property is nice—but a 10% gain on a property you financed at 20% down supercharges your return on the money you personally invested.

This can be a hard concept to grasp; it was for me at first, so I've created a chart to make it more clear. Here's a side-by-side look at two scenarios.

Scenario 1: Buy a $300,000 house with cash.

Scenario 2: Buy three $300,000 homes with $100,000 cash down payment and finance $200,000 on each. We will assume that each home rents for $3,000 per month (the 1% Rule again) and the properties are financed with a 30-year loan at 6%. After 30 years this is what it looks like:

Scenario		Total Rent Collected	Total Mortgage	Initial Cash	Net Profit
1 home	paid in cash	$1,080,000	$0	$300,000	$780,000
3 homes	each home: $100k downpymt	$3,240,000	$1,295,029	$300,000	$1,644,971

Even though you borrow and pay about $1.3 million in mortgage interest and principal over the years, the three-home strategy produces more than double the net profit of the single cash purchase.

Let's take it a step further to demonstrate the point. What if instead of putting down $100,000 on three houses, you put down $50,000 on six houses? What would that look like after 30 years (assuming the same 30-year loan at 6%)?

Scenario		Total Rent Collected	Total Mortgage	Initial Cash	Net Profit
1 home	paid in cash	$1,080,000	$0	$300,000	$780,000
6 homes	each home: $50k downpymt $250k financed	$6,480,000	$3,237,573	$300,000	$2,942,427

Cash *feels* safe but *grows* slower. Paying with cash and owning free and clear eliminates mortgage risk and interest, but you're limited to the income of just one property.

MIC DROP MOMENT

Cash is Queen,
but Leverage
multiplies wealth.

Cash is queen, but leverage multiplies wealth. If your goal is long-term wealth and you're comfortable managing more properties and debt, smart leverage may make more sense for you than cash. But if you value simplicity and no monthly payments, cash can still deliver steady income with less stress.

Leverage involves financing. Let's get into some of the ways you can finance your dreams.

Conventional Loans

♬ *Just Dance* ♬

Conventional loans are what most people think of when they hear "mortgage." These are backed by banks and credit unions. These are often the types of loans used to purchase primary residences and second homes.

When you're using a traditional (conventional) loan to buy an investment property, banks and lenders tighten the screws a bit compared to buying a primary residence. Hopefully, you're a homeowner, and if not, I get it, you have your reasons. Homeowners have been through the loan process before and know what to expect. It's tedious, you will be required to give a ton of documentation, and you will feel like your lender knows everything about your financial life.

She should! While getting a loan may be exhausting, wouldn't you want to make sure that someone was financially sound, able to pay you back and had strong, solid assets that you could access just in case they *didn't* pay you back? I know I would want that info if I were loaning out several hundred thousand dollars to someone *I didn't even know* and that's exactly what the bank is doing for you—loaning you a ton of money. Work with your lender and get them the needed docs as fast as you can. Over time, the process will become second nature.

Here's what they're looking for and what you need to have dialed in:

The Ideal Borrower

When you're using a traditional loan to buy an investment property, banks are going to look at you a little differently than if you were just purchasing your primary home. They know investment properties come with more risk, so their standards are tighter. Why is an investment house riskier? Because if you lose your job and can't make ends meet, banks know you are more likely to walk away from an investment property than the one that puts a roof over you and your family's heads. And they are right.

Here is what they're checking for:

Credit score. First up is your credit score. Most lenders want to see at least a 680, but you'll get better rates if you're sitting at 700 or higher. The lower your score, the higher your interest rate, and if it's too low you might get denied altogether. Not sure how to improve a low credit score? Go grab my first book and read up, sister.

Down payment. Next is your down payment. For investment properties, you're usually putting down *at least* 20% for single-family homes. Down payments may go up to 25–30% if you're going after a duplex, triplex, or fourplex. Since you're putting more money in up-front, the good news is you won't be dealing with those pesky PMI (private mortgage insurance) payments.

Debt-to-Income Ratio. Banks will also want to see a solid debt-to-income ratio (DTI), usually under 45%. That means all your monthly debts (like student loans, car payments, credit cards, and mortgages) need to stay within 45% of your gross income. These are the items that pop up on your credit report.

They are not looking for how much your utilities cost or what you spend on Amazon monthly (thank God).

Reserves. Another big one is reserves. Lenders want to know you've got a cushion in the bank in case things go sideways: like vacancies, repairs, or surprises. Typically, they want to see 2 to 6 months of PITIA (Principal, Interest, Taxes, Insurance, and HOA) saved up for *each* property you own.

Income. As for income, you'll need to show W2s or tax returns. If you're self-employed, they'll want to see at least two years of stable income. If you're planning to use the property's rental income to help you qualify, some lenders will count 75% of projected rent based on an appraiser's estimate or a signed lease. Others might want to see that you've already reported rental income on your tax returns, especially if you've been in the game for a while.

The Bank's Ideal Borrower

Requirement	Minimum for Approval	Ideal for Best Terms
Credit Score	680	740
Down Payment	15–25%	25%
DTI Ratio	<45%	<36%
Reserves	2–6 months (per property)	6+ months
Rental Income	May use 75% of market rent	Current Schedule E rental income
Property Condition	Move-in ready	Turnkey, no rehab needed

Don't be fooled by websites that say you can put your property in an LLC and not use your credit. At the beginning, and for quite some time while you build your portfolio, your personal credit will be tied to the loan, usually in the form of a personal guarantee.

> **ROCKSTAR TIP**
> Keep your credit score and your debt-to-income ratio healthy. Lenders love stability.

That means you are responsible to pay back the loan, and if you don't, the bank can come after you and your assets. Check with your state to see what that looks like. In Florida, for example, if you default on an investment property, your primary residence is still protected from claims. In other states, it's different. In Georgia, for example, your primary residence is only protected up to $10,000. That means if you bail on an investment property, the bank can take back the house AND come after your other assets if they haven't gotten back all their money.

Get a CPA or attorney to explain this to you in legal terms. Set up your properties in ways that protect you. (I'll talk more about this at the end of this chapter).

For a conventional loan, the property itself matters, too. It's gotta be livable—no major issues like a bad roof, broken HVAC, or missing bathrooms. If you're buying a multi-family, expect a more detailed appraisal and sometimes a rent analysis to back up your numbers.

I have people ask me frequently about bidding at foreclosure or other auctions. You won't be able to use a conventional loan to do this. These homes will require cash at the auction and frequently these homes are not livable. Be prepared to pay additional cash for renovations. Only *after* you renovate the home can you "cash-out" refinance into a conventional loan.

And finally; intent matters. You've got to be up-front about your plans. If you tell your lender you're buying a "second home" but then list it on Airbnb right after you close, you're technically violating the loan agreement. Lenders can check up on that, especially if something goes wrong with the loan. Lenders aren't idiots, so don't treat them like they are. Shoot it straight; karma is always watching.

In short, when it comes to investment loans, you need to demonstrate to the bank you're financially solid, serious about the deal, and that the property makes sense as an investment. Treat it like a business loan because that's exactly what it is.

There are other things to consider when getting a conventional loan. Here's a breakdown of the key rules, strategies, and sneaky little nuances when it comes to conventional loans, how many you can have, what banks are looking for, and how to play the game like a pro.

How Many Conventional Loans Can You Have?

Per Bank: There's *technically* no limit to how many mortgages you can have with one bank, but most banks will cap it at around 4–5 loans per borrower to manage their own risk. Even if you're a rockstar client, they don't want too much exposure with one person.

In Your Personal Name (Across All Lenders): Fannie Mae and Freddie Mac allow up to ten conventional residential loans in your personal name. The first four will be pretty straightforward. Once you hit loans five through ten, things get trickier and will likely require:

- Higher credit score requirements (usually 720+)
- Larger down payments (25% or more)
- Tighter debt-to-income ratios
- Increased reserves (typically 6 months per property)

I really want to be able to say to you, *Never put investment property loans in your personal name!* And sure, that's great advice ... in theory. But let's be real. When you're just getting started, it's not always that simple or practical. While "gurus" may shun me for this potentially risky move, my goal will always be to be real with you.

Those self-proclaimed "experts" commonly acquire properties very differently from the way most of us approach it. They're teaching from a stage or a podcast, not standing at a closing table trying to scrape together a 25% down payment or get a decent rate. They might have access to private lenders, partnerships, or fancy legal teams, and that's great for them, but it's not always the reality for a new Boss Lady investor trying to buy her first or second property.

The truth is most investors I know, including many successful ones, have one or several loans in their personal name. It's how they got their foot in the door. It's often the most accessible way to start building your portfolio, especially if you're using conventional financing.

That said, Boss Ladies should always go in with eyes wide open. Yes, there are risks to holding property in your personal name, like liability exposure or the impact on your credit report if something goes sideways. But that doesn't mean it's a deal-breaker. It just means you need to protect yourself in other ways. That could mean setting up a strong insurance policy, keeping solid reserves, or creating an umbrella policy to shield your personal assets.

The point is, don't let perfect be the enemy of progress. Don't wait to have the "perfect" LLC structure or the ideal financing plan before you make your move. Start where you are, do it smart, and grow from there. You'll learn, evolve, and restructure along the way, just like every investor who's come before you. Make sure that you are playing the game in a way that is comfortable for you.

The goal isn't to follow a guru, it's to build a life you love, one smart investment at a time.

What Happens After Ten Bank Loans?

At that point, you've outgrown conventional lending. Congrats, you're a legit real estate mogul! You'll need to start using:

- Portfolio loans through small local banks or credit unions.
- Commercial loans (especially for multi-family or mixed-use).
- DSCR (Debt Service Coverage Ratio) loans, which qualify based on property cash flow, not your personal income.

Or, once your business has built solid credit of its own, you can start buying properties under your LLC, letting your business help fund your next investment.

Which Banks Offer the Best Deals for Conventional Loans?

> **ROCKSTAR TIP**
> Don't let one "NO" from a lender stop you. Shop around.

With so many financial institutions to choose from, you have many choices for financing your deals. Here's a cheat sheet:

Types of Lenders

Lender Type	Best For	Why
Credit Unions	First-time buyers, lower fees	Often more flexible underwriting and low origination fees
Local/Regional Banks	Relationship-based investing	You can develop a personal relationship and negotiate more
Mortgage Brokers	Comparing rates across multiple lenders	They shop your loan around to find best pricing
National Banks	Convenience, brand trust	May offer fewer products but streamlined processes

Build a relationship with your lender like they're your business partner. A trusted lender will go to bat for you, help you structure deals creatively, and even speed things up when time is tight.

> **ROCKSTAR TIP**
> Build a relationship with your lender like they're your business partner.

Second Home vs. Investment Property

♫ *Cheek to Cheek* ♫

Another topic that comes up when looking at conventional loans is second home loans. These are loans used to purchase homes that you would use as your "second" home. The beach house that you don't rent out. The ski-chalet for family vacations (again, that you *don't* rent out).

Second home loans have many similarities in requirements and rates to conventional loans for investment properties; however, there are a few differences to keep in mind when obtaining a loan for either a second home or investment property.

Feature	Second Home	Investment Property
Usage	Must be occupied by you part of the year	Used to generate rental income
Down Payment	As low as 10%	Typically 15–25%
Interest Rate	May be lower depending on market	Higher (lenders see more risk)
Rental Use	Not supposed to rent it out full-time	Higher (lenders see more risk)
Location	Must be far enough from primary home (usually 50+ miles)	No distance requirement

What if you buy a second home ... then use it as a rental?

This is where it gets spicy.

Let's say you buy a beach house as a "second home" with a low down payment and lower interest rate, but then turn around and rent it out on Airbnb. Is that ... illegal?

Technically, it probably violates the loan agreement.

The second home rider you signed states you *intend to* occupy the home personally. But guess what? Intent is hard to prove unless you're blatantly misrepresenting yourself. Lenders rarely police how the property is used *after* closing unless there's fraud involved. They want to get paid, bottom line.

We bought our first vacation home as just that: a vacation home for us to use and enjoy. We renovated it and then decided to try out Airbnb, just to see. Obviously, we know how that turned out.

Could our bank have called the loan? Yes. Would they? No. They didn't (nor have they ever) because we were making our payments and keeping the asset valuable (by making it even nicer).

At the time we purchased that first vacation house, we didn't even know the difference between a second home loan and an investment loan.

My advice, be honest. I actually did call my lender to let them know what we were doing. They told me to make the payments, and they would never bother me. And they haven't.

♬ *A Star is Born* ♬

If you're buying your very first property, an FHA loan might be your golden ticket. Backed by the Federal Housing Administration, these loans are designed to help people with lower credit scores or smaller down payments.

FHA Loans

Government Hooker

Don't worry, you do not have to be an actual hooker, but you will be taking advantage of a government-backed product when you use an FHA Loan. These loans are backed by the Federal Housing Administration (that's the F, H and A) which is part of the Department of Housing and Urban Development (that's the H, U and D in the "HUD" forms we discussed).

Here's the scenario: you're ready to buy an investment property and you've heard whispers about FHA loans being a great way to get your foot in the real estate door. You're not wrong. FHA loans can be a total game-changer for Boss Ladies like us, especially if you're working with limited savings or you've hit a few bumps in your credit journey. But before you dive in, let's talk about who qualifies for one. IMO, they are a great way to get started in investing with the bank shouldering more risk.

Credit Score. The beautiful thing about FHA loans is that they're more forgiving than conventional loans when it comes to your credit score. While *most* lenders prefer to see a score of 580 or higher, you can still qualify with a score as low as 500, you'll just need to put more money down. With a score of 580 or above, you could qualify with as little as 3.5% down. If your score is between 500 and 579, the FHA requires a 10% down payment. Lenders can have their own stricter rules on top of FHA's guidelines, so it pays to shop around and find one that understands your unique story.

Down Payment. You'll need to have your down payment ready, but the good news is that FHA loans are flexible about where that money comes from. Your down payment can come from your own savings or be gifted to you by a family member, nonprofit, or even your employer. Just make sure you can document it properly, since lenders love paper trails.

One of the most beautiful things about an FHA loan is the lower down payment. If your credit score is 580 or higher, you can buy a house with as little as 3.5% down. If your score is lower than that, you can possibly still qualify with a higher down payment. Boss Lady, real talk: If your credit score is lower than 580, work on your credit score before diving into real estate investing (*Becoming a Boss Lady Investor* covers how to do this).

Income. You don't need to be rolling in cash, but the FHA wants to know you have a steady job or consistent income. Typically, lenders like to see two years of employment in the same field. If you're self-employed, you can still qualify, you'll just need to provide two years of tax returns to reveal your income is reliable. The key here is consistency. They want to see that you can reasonably make your monthly payments if the rents are not coming in.

Debt-to-Income Ratio. Speaking of payments, one of the numbers lenders look closely at is your debt-to-income ratio, or DTI. This is a fancy way of saying: how much of your income is already spoken for? FHA guidelines generally allow up to 43% of your gross income to go toward your total debts (this includes your new mortgage, student loans, credit cards, car payments, etc.). In some cases, they'll even allow up to 50% if you have strong compensating factors, like an excellent credit score or extra cash reserves.

Other Requirements. Another key requirement is that you're planning to live in the property as your primary residence.

FHA loans aren't for vacation homes or investment properties, at least not right away. (But if you're thinking house hack buying a multi-unit home and living in one unit while renting out the others, FHA says, go for it. You can still qualify if you live in one of the units.)

You'll also need to be a U.S. citizen, permanent resident, or non-permanent resident with a valid Social Security number. The home itself must also meet certain standards. The FHA wants to make sure the property is safe and livable, so if the roof is falling in or the wiring is sketchy, you might have to make repairs or use a special type of FHA loan, like the 203(k), which wraps renovation costs into your mortgage.

Oh, and let's not forget about loan limits. FHA loans aren't designed for luxury homes; they're intended to help regular folks buy reasonably priced properties. Each county has a loan limit based on local home prices, so be sure to check what applies to your area.

And we cannot forget about PMI.

PMI (Private Mortgage Insurance) is a monthly insurance premium that protects the lender, not the borrower, if you stop making payments on your loan. It's typically required on conventional loans when you put down less than 20%, and FHA loans always include mortgage insurance (called MIP) because of their low down payment requirements, ensuring lenders are protected while helping buyers get into homes with as little as 3.5% down.

Lastly, let's talk about the not-so-glamorous stuff: bankruptcies and foreclosures. If you've had one, don't panic. You can still qualify for an FHA loan; it just depends on how long it's been. Generally, you'll need to wait two years after a

Chapter 7 bankruptcy is discharged and three years after a foreclosure. During that time, it's all about rebuilding. Show that you've paid your bills on time, kept your debt manageable, and bounced back with grace.

Remember the story about my hubby's townhouse? He used an FHA loan when he purchased that property.

The best part? You don't have to start with a six-figure income or a huge savings account either. And that's what I want you to take away from this: you don't have to wait until everything is perfect to take your first step.

VA Loans

Served Our Country? Then There Are A
🎶 Million Reasons 🎶 You Deserve This Benefit

If you (or your spouse) have served in the military, first, thank you for your service. Second, please make sure you know about one of the best real estate financing tools out there: the VA loan.

VA loans are backed by the U.S. Department of Veterans Affairs, and they're designed to help service members, veterans, and eligible surviving spouses buy homes with incredible terms. Think of them as the VIP pass to homeownership—no down payment required, no private mortgage insurance (PMI), and often lower interest rates than conventional loans.

Why VA Loans Are Amazing

Here's why this program is such a win for qualified borrowers:

- **0% down payment.** You can buy a home without putting a penny down. That means keeping your savings intact for repairs, furnishings, or your next investment.
- **No PMI.** Unlike FHA or conventional loans, you won't pay monthly mortgage insurance, even with no down payment. That alone can save hundreds of dollars per month.
- **Competitive interest rates.** Because the loan is guaranteed by the VA, lenders offer more favorable rates.
- **Flexible credit requirements.** You don't need perfect credit to qualify.
- **No prepayment penalty:** If you want to make extra payments and pay off early (hello, equity!), you can.

How VA Loans Work

VA loans are issued by private lenders, like banks, credit unions, or mortgage companies, but the VA guarantees a portion of the loan. That means if the borrower defaults, the lender is protected, which makes them more willing to offer favorable terms.

The home you buy has to be your primary residence, but here's a fun tip: you can purchase a multi-unit property (up to four units) with a VA loan, as long as you live in one of them. Yep, that means a VA house hack is totally possible. Live in one unit, rent out the others, and let your tenants help cover your mortgage while you build wealth.

A Few Things to Know

VA funding fee. This helps keep the program running. It's usually rolled into your loan and varies based on your down payment and whether you've used a VA loan before.

Qualifications. You'll still need to qualify based on income, credit, and debt-to-income ratio.

Appraisal standards. The property must meet VA appraisal standards which focus on safety, livability, and soundness (basically making sure you're not buying a total money pit).

If you or your partner qualify, the VA loan is one of the most powerful tools available for getting into real estate with little to no money down. It's not just for buying your "forever home" ... it can also be a stepping stone into investing if you choose the right property.

Whether you're a veteran yourself or you're married to one, don't leave this benefit on the table. You earned it, and it could be the key that unlocks your first (or next) investment property.

Chapter 8

CREATIVE FINANCING

🎶 Do What U Want 🎶

Sometimes, the most powerful tool you have is creativity. Girl, I am the (self-proclaimed) Queen of Creative Financing. Deals don't always come to life when you are expecting them, so you must be willing to think outside the box. Perhaps a deal ends up in your lap and for whatever reason you can't qualify for a loan or just don't *want* to deal with one. Here are some out-of-the-box financing strategies that real investors use every day:

Home Equity Line of Credit (HELOC)

🎶 Beautiful, Dirty, Rich 🎶

We've touched on HELOCs already a bit in the book but let's do a quick refresher.

A HELOC, or "Home Equity Line of Credit", is essentially a revolving credit line backed by the equity you've already built in a property. Think of it as giving your home a credit card with a big limit and a lower interest rate than most consumer debt. They are beautiful and have helped propel me from doing good to boss lady status. And yes, I did get dirty along the way as I tore down tiles, gutted bathrooms and painted more walls than I ever thought I would.

Equity is simply the current market value of your property minus what you still owe on the mortgage. For example, if your home is worth $400,000 and you owe $250,000, you have $150,000 in equity. A lender will typically allow you to borrow up to about 75–85% of the home's value, including your existing mortgage. If the bank approves 80% loan-to-value on that $400,000 property, the total debt allowed is $320,000. Subtract your current mortgage balance ($250,000) and you could access roughly $70,000 as a credit line.

Once approved, you enter a draw period, usually the first five to ten years, during which you can borrow, repay, and borrow again up to your limit. You typically make interest-only payments on whatever amount you actually draw. After the draw period ends, the line closes and you begin repaying both principal and interest over the remaining term, often another ten to twenty years.

For real estate investors, a HELOC can be a game-changer. You can pull funds from the line and use them as down payments or even full cash offers on new deals. That might mean taking $60,000 from your HELOC to cover the 20% down payment on a $300,000 rental and financing the rest with a traditional mortgage, or using it as short-term "bridge financing" to buy and renovate a property quickly before refinancing into a long-term loan. Because you only pay interest on what you draw, the HELOC offers flexibility and speed that can help you compete in hot markets.

The advantages are clear: you gain quick access to capital, you typically enjoy lower rates than credit cards or unsecured loans, and you're leveraging assets you already own to build additional income streams.

But the power comes with responsibility. HELOCs often carry variable interest rates that can rise over time, and because your property is collateral, defaulting could lead to foreclosure. The key is to treat a HELOC like business capital: calculate carefully, plan for rate changes, and make sure the cash flow from any new investment comfortably covers the payments. Used wisely, a HELOC can turn the equity in one property into the funding source for the next, helping you expand your portfolio without waiting years to save another down payment.

Private Money

Friends with (Financial) Benefits

♬ *Hold My Hand* ♬

Private money is exactly what it sounds like: real people (not banks) loaning you money to do your deal. Think friends, family, mentors, or investors who want a return on their money but don't want to do the work.

Borrowing private money, especially from a friend or family member, can be a great way to fund a real estate deal without going through a traditional lender, but it comes with *serious* responsibility.

Private lenders often charge higher interest rates than banks (think 12–15% or more), which makes sense, they're taking on a big risk by investing in *you*. Here's a hard truth that you need to pay extra attention to when working with friends: if you don't do your due diligence and make sure the numbers work, you're not just jeopardizing a deal, you're putting a personal relationship on the line.

Imagine sitting across from your friend at dinner, knowing you owe them tens of thousands of dollars and can't pay it back. Awkward doesn't even begin to cover it. That's why you must treat private money with the same seriousness as a bank loan, if not more. Run your numbers. Double-check your exit strategy. Build in a cushion for surprises. Because at the end of the day, your reputation and your friendships are more valuable than any one deal.

How to make it work:

- Build trust (have a business plan, not just a dream)
- Be professional (treat it like a business, because it is)
- Offer them a return—interest, a share of profits, or equity

You're not begging for money; you're offering an opportunity. Remember that.

Private money can be one of the most powerful tools in your investing arsenal, but only if you handle it with care, integrity, and respect. My business partner and I use private money all the time to fund our deals, and one of our most consistent lenders is a longtime friend of hers. When we were just getting started, we treated that first loan like a professional pitch. We built out a detailed presentation of the numbers, made sure every projection was backed by real data, put him on the deed with us to give him security, and checked in every month with updates. We had to prove that we were worthy of the risk.

Fast forward to today, and the trust is so strong that if she calls him tomorrow, he'll wire us hundreds of thousands of dollars within a week. And here's the interesting part—these days he's my friend too, and I'm usually the one who sources and drives the deals. But she still must make the call.

Why?

Because they're both Vietnamese, and in their culture, trust and family ties are deeply intertwined. Even though I'm fully trusted, the comfort and familiarity of that cultural connection matters. And we respect that, because honoring relationships is what keeps the doors open.

That same principle came to life in one of the most meaningful deals I've ever been a part of—the purchase of my parents' dream beach house. It was everything they'd ever wanted: oceanfront, zoned for vacation rentals, and located in the same town where they honeymooned ***fifty-two*** years earlier. And on this deal, I wasn't simply their daughter, but I was also their realtor. For a variety of reasons, at the eleventh hour, when they were just about to close on the home, the bank pulled out. Just one day before closing, we were told the lender was out and it would likely take up to *six months* to close the loan with a new lender.

There was no way the seller was going to wait that long.

That's when my reputation became more valuable than anything in my bank account. The lender, who was a friend of mine, who knew the property and trusted my instincts, ran the numbers with me. It was a solid deal with equity and income potential. So, he called *his* friend, a private lender I'd never even met, and vouched for me. I'm not exaggerating when I say that the man he called wired us **one million dollars** the very next day so my parents could buy their dream home. I co-signed on the loan (a prerequisite since it was based on my reputation), we closed on time, and we paid him back ***in full*** within six months (after securing a new lender-based mortgage).

That house now generates nearly $200,000 a year in vacation rental income; is worth over a million dollars more than we paid and allows my parents to spend their golden years enjoying the beach, making memories with the grandbabies and renting it out when they aren't there to cover the costs.

The moral? Your name is the most valuable thing you own. If you build a reputation as someone who honors your word, pays people back, and delivers what you promise, money will find you. Not just once, but again and again. People will offer to lend to you before you even ask. That's the power of relationships. That's the power of private money. And that's the power of doing the right thing every single time.

Hard Money

♬ *Look What I Found* ♬

Hard money lenders are real estate's version of high-interest speed dating. They move fast, fund fast, and care more about the deal than your credit score. They're basically private money but from people you don't know, aren't connected to and/or who do this as a business.

Hard money loans are often confused with private money, but they're quite different. While private money typically comes from someone you know, like a friend, colleague, or trusted contact, hard money comes from a professional lender or investment group. They are often found online, through investment groups or via referrals. These lenders don't care as much about your credit score or employment history. What they *do* care about is the asset: the property itself. Hard money loans are asset-based, which means they're primarily focused on the value of the property and the potential for profit. These loans are short-term, high-interest, and often come with hefty fees and requirements, things like interest-only payments and holding periods before you can refinance. But when traditional financing or private lenders aren't an option, and a great deal is on the line, hard money can be the bridge that gets you from stuck to successful.

I'll never forget the first time I took out a hard money loan. Another one of my business partners and I had found a dilapidated property in an *amazing* location, one of those rare gems that, if done right, could be transformed into a high-performing vacation rental. The only problem? We were already under contract for two other properties and didn't have the cash on hand to pull off a third. We were stretched thin but didn't want to let this opportunity slip away. So, we started searching online and found a hard money lender somewhere across the country. I can't even remember where they were located, that's how impersonal it was.

At the time, interest rates were around 4% (oh, the good old days), but this loan came with an 8.5% rate and a requirement to hold it for a year before refinancing. The terms weren't cheap, but we crunched the numbers and decided to go for it.

We bought the house for $242,500. The lender agreed to finance $182,500, and we paid over $13,000 in closing costs, which may seem high but let's be real, these lenders charge a lot to take on this type of risk. My partner and I scraped together the remaining $73,000 and paid interest-only payments for the year which we offset with rental income once the renovations were complete. We then invested another $40,000 *each* into renovations, bringing the property up to high-end rental standards. A year later, we "cash-out" refinanced into a commercial loan for $224,000 at just 5%. We actually could've taken significantly more on the loan, up to $400,000 in fact, but we chose to stay conservative for strategic reasons. We paid off the $182,500 hard money loan and reimbursed ourselves $21,000 each, leaving us with an investment of around $55,500 each in the property.

Today, that house is worth over $700,000. It rents out like crazy, bringing in over $80,000 a year in income. A few years after our refinance, as the home continued to appreciate, we took out another loan for $70,000 to install a pool and elevate the guest experience even more.

Now here's the kicker: assuming a modest 3% annual appreciation, by the time I am ready to sell in about seven years, the home could be worth over $900,000. From our initial investment of about $55,500 each, that's a return of over 300%-*per person*. That first hard money loan was scary. The interest rate was high, the timeline was tight, and the pressure was on. But taking the leap, running the numbers, and believing in the vision paid off in a big way.

When used strategically, hard money loans can unlock deals that would otherwise be impossible. They're not for the faint of heart, and they're definitely not for every situation, but when the deal is solid and you've done your homework, they can open doors to massive long-term wealth.

Hard Money Loans are Best for:

- Flips or BRRRRs (Buy, Rehab, Rent, Refinance, Repeat)
- When you need money *yesterday*
- Investors with a solid plan and exit strategy

Don't be surprised if you are asked to personally guarantee a hard-money loan. Even though the asset is what backs the loan, most hard money lenders I know still require a personal guarantee on these loans. They won't appear on your credit (unless you default), but you will likely be personally responsible for the loan.

Be aware, interest rates can be high on these loans, 12%-15% or more, and loans are short-term. But when used strategically they can be the rocket fuel to scale fast.

Partnerships

Teamwork Makes the Dream Work
♬ *You and I* ♬

Don't have all the skills (or cash) needed for a deal? Bring in a partner who does. You bring the hustle; they bring the capital. Or maybe you handle the deal, and they handle renovations. Just be sure to get everything in writing.

Boss Lady Reminder: Equity is expensive—if you can afford to borrow money and keep 100% of the deal, that's often better long-term. But when the deal is big and you need a squad? Partnerships are the way to go.

Partnering Up: The Good, The Bad, and The Must-Knows

Real estate partnerships can be an incredible way to grow your portfolio faster, pool resources, and share the workload, but they're not always sunshine and cash flow. Especially when you're partnering with friends or acquaintances, it's essential to go in with eyes wide open.

> **ROCKSTAR TIP**
> Sharing equity is expensive. But a *good* deal with a partner is better than no deal at all.

If you've been reading closely (and I hope you have), you've probably noticed just how often partnerships come up in this book. That's because partnerships have been one of the most critical tools I've used to scale my real estate portfolio and grow my businesses. From flipping houses to building out vacation rentals to funding multi-family deals, I've rarely done it alone. But let me be crystal clear: partnerships are not something to take lightly. I've had ex-friends sue me. I've been burned. So yes, while I now have what I call my dream team of investment partners, a solid crew of people I trust with my money and my name, it took time, mistakes, and a few painful lessons to get here.

These days, people literally reach out and ask how they can partner with me because they know if I'm involved, the deal is probably solid. My answer? Bring me a winner. If you've got a deal that makes sense, let's talk. After my first book, *Becoming a Boss Lady Investor*, I had women come out of the woodwork asking how we could work together. I've been blessed to be able to partner with some incredible Boss Ladies and Boss Ladies-in-the-making to increase all our bottom lines. The truth is, I'm always looking for great opportunities, and if I can pull another Boss Lady up the ladder while I'm climbing, even better.

But, and this is a big one, *you've* got to bring something to the table. That might be money. But in the beginning, more often than not, it's time, labor, hustle, and follow-through. Maybe you're the one scraping popcorn ceilings, painting walls, handling spreadsheets, or managing contractors. Just please don't come to a partnership expecting the other person to do it all while you ride the equity train. And, once you commit, hold yourself accountable. If you said you'd be there at 8 a.m. to paint, be there at 7:45 a.m. with coffee and rollers in hand. When you do that, people take notice. That's how teams are formed. That's how reputations are built. And that's how your name gets passed around in all the right rooms. A good partner sees effort, integrity, and consistency and when you find that magic match, you'll want to work together again and again.

The Good:

A partnership can allow you to buy a bigger or better property than you could afford on your own. You can divide the responsibilities, maybe one person manages the rehab while the other handles the finances or tenant communication. You might also benefit from different skill sets, one of you might be detail-oriented while the other is a big-picture thinker. If your partnership is well-structured, aligned, and mutually respectful, it can be a dream team.

The Bad:

Money and pressure have a funny way of revealing people's true colors. If you go in without clear agreements, defined roles, or aligned goals, things can get messy fast. One person might want to sell early, while the other wants to hold for long-term cash flow. One partner might start ghosting when things get tough, leaving the other with all the responsibility. Or worse, someone could make poor decisions that impact both your finances and your friendship.

The Must-Knows:

Before entering any partnership, especially with someone you know socially, take the time to review these critical pieces:

- Clear financial contributions: Who's bringing what to the table? Are you splitting 50/50 or based on what each person invests? If you don't have as much money as your partner, what are you contributing to offset that and how is that measured?
- Defined roles and responsibilities: Who handles what? Property management? Bookkeeping? Repairs?
- Exit strategy: What happens if one person wants out? How will the property be sold, bought out, or refinanced?
- Aligned goals and values: Do you both want cash flow? Appreciation? A long-term hold or quick flip?
- Personality fit: Can you communicate openly? Can they handle conflict like an adult? Do you trust them to follow through?

And please, please, put it all in writing. An operating agreement, a partnership contract-something official.

At the end of the day, real estate partnerships can be an incredible tool or a fast track to resentment and regret. Choose your partners as carefully as you choose your properties, and you'll protect your investment, your peace of mind, and your relationships.

MIC DROP MOMENT

Trust is good, but contracts are better.

Self-Directed IRA

The Edge of Glory

Most people think an IRA is a boring box where you stash money and let Wall Street shuffle it around. Most people wouldn't be entirely wrong. But a self-directed IRA flips that script and puts *you* in control.

A self-directed IRA is a special type of retirement plan that lets you invest your retirement funds in a much wider range of assets. Traditional IRAs, 401(k) plans, and Roth IRAs typically have limited investment options like stocks, bonds, mutual funds or index funds.

With a self-directed IRA, you can invest in other alternatives like *real estate,* private lending, tax liens, startups and precious metals.

While there are differences in investment options, you still have the choice of making tax-deferred contributions (like a traditional IRA) or after tax contributions (like a Roth IRA).

There are very strict rules that you must follow when using a self-directed IRA. The IRS has "prohibited transactions" that cannot be a part of your investments. When you invest through a self-directed IRA, all the money inside that account, and anything it earns, belongs to your retirement account, not *you personally* (yet).

That means you can absolutely build wealth, earn profits, and grow your portfolio within the IRA, but you can't personally use or benefit from the investment *until you retire and start taking withdrawals*, and you must keep all expenses and income inside the IRA. There are also paperwork and costs including setup fees, annual maintenance, and the need for a savvy custodian to stay compliant.

Lastly, just like any IRA, your money is still retirement money and pulling it out before retirement age can trigger penalties and taxes.

Because self-directed IRAs havec omplex rules that must be followed to a tee, you will want to consult with a custodian for one of these plans *before* you purchase any real estate to put into your retirement account.

Seller Financing

♬ *Free Woman* ♬

With this type of financing, the seller acts as the bank. You pay them directly over time. Down payments vary by seller. These are great for motivated sellers who want passive income and investors that don't want to go through a bank.

Seller financing can be a powerful tool in your real estate investing toolkit, but like anything, it comes with both benefits and risks. On the plus side, seller financing can make deals happen when traditional lenders say no, especially if you have less-than-perfect credit or need a creative financing option. It often allows for more flexible terms, faster closings, and fewer up-front costs since you're working directly with the seller instead of a bank. Plus, there's room to negotiate everything from the interest rate to the repayment schedule.

But there are downsides too. Interest rates may be higher than conventional loans, and if the seller still has a mortgage on the property (called a "wraparound"), things can get complicated, or even risky, if the seller is not making their payments. There's also typically a shorter loan term or a balloon payment, which means you might need to refinance or pay off the balance in full in just a few years. Like any deal, make sure to have a solid contract, and you should make sure to consult with a great real estate attorney before jumping in.

Lease-To-Own

Lease-to-own, also called rent-to-own, is one of the most underrated creative financing tools in real estate. It's a strategy that lets a tenant *become* a buyer over time, and it gives an investor (that's you, Boss Lady!) a powerful way to maximize profit, reduce vacancy, and help someone else achieve homeownership. It's a win-win when done right.

Here's how it works: instead of a traditional rental agreement, your tenant signs a lease plus an option agreement giving them the right (but not the obligation) to purchase the property at a predetermined price within a certain timeframe, usually 1–3 years. The tenant typically pays an option fee up front (often 1–5% of the purchase price), which is nonrefundable but applied toward their down payment if they go through with the purchase. Each month, they may also pay a slight rent premium, a portion of which you can credit toward their eventual purchase.

Lease-to-own can be a great tool if:

- You want steady cash flow and a higher-quality tenant who has skin in the game.
- You're not ready to buy immediately but want to lock in a future price, especially in a rising market (if you are the buyer) OR you are not ready to sell immediately but want to lock in a future price in a declining market (if you are the seller).
- The home needs time for appreciation or minor upgrades before a traditional sale makes sense.
- You want to avoid paying agent commissions and sell directly to your tenant.
- A potential buyer needs time to repair credit, save more cash, or stabilize income.

From the investor side, lease-to-own can dramatically increase your returns: you collect the option fee up front, earn above-market rent during the lease period, and often still get market value (or better if the market happens to decline) when they buy. And if the tenant decides not to purchase? You keep the option fee, keep your rent premiums, and start again with a new tenant or traditional sale.

From the buyer-tenant side, this approach gives people a much-needed bridge when life or finances aren't quite perfect yet. You're offering not just a place to live, but a pathway to ownership, something that can change families for generations.

Lease-to-own is not for every property or every tenant, but when layered into your investing toolkit, it's a powerful creative strategy that can increase your income, reduce turnover, and give you more control over how and when you sell. And for many investors, including me, it's one of those hidden gems that just quietly prints money when set up correctly.

DSCR Loans

Loans That May Earn Your
🎶 Applause 🎶

A DSCR loan, short for "Debt Service Coverage Ratio" loan, is a tool real estate investors can use to qualify for a mortgage based on a property's income, not their own. Instead of looking at pay stubs and tax returns, the lender looks at how much money the property brings in and whether it can cover the loan payment.

Here's how it works: the lender calculates the DSCR by dividing the property's Net Operating Income (after expenses, before debt) by the total monthly debt payment. If the property brings in $2,000 a month and your mortgage costs $1,600, your DSCR is 1.25, which tells the lender the property is making 25% more than the debt costs. That's a green light.

DSCR loans are especially helpful if you're self-employed, have already maxed out your conventional loans, or want to buy properties under an LLC. They skip the traditional income checks, which can make the process faster and more flexible.

The trade-off? You'll usually pay a higher interest rate and need a bigger down payment, and the property *must* cash flow well. If the income isn't there, the loan won't work.

While it's not always the cheapest option, a DSCR loan can be a powerful tool to help you grow your portfolio when traditional financing starts to limit your options.

"Subject To" Deals

🎶 *Born this Way* 🎶

A "Subject To"" deal, short for "Subject To the Existing Financing," is a creative real estate strategy where you, as the buyer, take control of a property subject to the seller's existing mortgage staying in place. You don't formally assume the loan; instead, the seller's loan remains in their name, but you make the payments on their behalf. This can be a powerful way to acquire property with little or no money down, no credit check, and no need for a traditional loan. It's especially useful when a seller is facing foreclosure or needs to move fast and just wants out of the financial burden.

While the buyer gets the benefits of ownership and control, the loan remains tied to the seller's credit, which can be a big risk for the seller if payments aren't made as promised. There's also the chance the lender could call the loan due under the "due-on-sale" clause, though this doesn't often happen. "Subject To" deals can be a win-win when done right, but they require trust, transparency, and strong legal documentation to protect both parties.

Remember my friend's son in Chapter 5? That was a "subject-to" deal. He was in over his head barreling towards foreclosure when I stepped in. We structured the deal so that I took over the mortgage payments, brought the property current, and handled all the renovations. The loan stayed in his name, but I took control of the property, made the payments, and had full authority to improve and eventually sell it.

1031 Exchange

The Power of 1031 Exchanges
♬ *Love Game* ♬

We briefly touched on one of the greatest wealth-building tools available to real estate investors, the 1031 Exchange, in Chapter 3. But this amazing tool can truly help Boss Ladies level-up their investments while taking advantage of tax codes that allow for tax-deferral. As a refresher, a 1031 Exchange lets you roll the gains from one investment property into another *without* paying capital gains taxes at the time of the sale. When used strategically, a 1031 can supercharge your portfolio growth, protect your profits, and help you trade up into bigger, better-performing assets.

Think of a 1031 Exchange as a "save and scale" button for real estate investors. You keep your money working *in the market*, instead of handing a chunk of it over to the IRS.

So, what exactly *is* a 1031 Exchange?

As I shared earlier, a 1031 Exchange (named after Section 1031 of the Internal Revenue Code) allows you to sell one investment property and purchase another "like-kind" investment property without paying capital gains taxes today.

Here are some key points to know when looking at doing a 1031 Exchange.

Investment property requirement. Both the property you sell *and* the property you buy must be investment or business properties (you can't use this strategy for your personal home).
"Like-kind" requirement. This doesn't mean identical. You can exchange:

- a rental house for a duplex
- a condo for a beach house rental
- land for an apartment building
- a short-term rental for a long-term rental

As long as the purpose is investment, it qualifies!

How a 1031 Exchange Works (Step-by-Step)

How do you go about using a 1031 Exchange? Here's the real world step-by-step flow.

Step 1. Decide to Exchange

You have a real estate investment that has equity—perhaps because you have been holding it for a while and there has been appreciation. Maybe you did a flip and built in equity. However you did it (congrats), you have a property that has equity that you decide you want to sell. For me, I like to build equity in a small property, then use the equity for a down payment on a bigger property ... I'll give you an example in just a few. Anyway, you also determine you want to defer capital gains and roll your profit into a new investment.

Step 2. Hire a Qualified Intermediary (QI)

In order to do a 1031 Exchange, you must hire a Qualified Intermediary before closing on the sale of your property. A QI is a neutral third party who will hold the proceeds from your sale and ensure the IRS rules are followed. I would start looking for a QI in your area long before the sale as they can be surprisingly hard to find *and* they charge fees that you will want to be prepared for.

Step 3. Sell Your Investment Property

At closing, the funds **cannot** come to you. Do not let the closing team wire the funds to your account. They must go directly to the QI.

Step 4. Identify Replacement Properties (45-Day Rule)

From the day you close on the sale, you have **45 days** to identify potential replacement properties. You can choose up to:

- Three properties of any value, OR
- More than three properties, as long as their combined value does not exceed 200% of the property you sold.

I'll go into more detail on this in a bit, but let's finish the steps first.

Step 5. Purchase the Replacement Property (180-Day Rule)

You must close on the replacement property *within 180 days* of selling the original property. Keep in mind the title of the sold property and the purchased property must be identical. If you were on the original title solo, you can't add someone else to the new title or put the new title in an LLC. It must be exactly the same as the title of the sold property.

I am working with a 1031 Exchange buyer right now. She was considering putting the new property in her LLC's name, but the old property was in her name. I'm so glad she shared that with me so I could help stop her from a costly mistake. That is the value of working with someone who understands this space.

Step 6. Execute the Exchange

Your Qualified Intermediary transfers the funds from your sale to the closing agent of the replacement property. Taxes are deferred, and you're now the proud owner of your next investment, tax bill delayed!

The 45-Day Identification Rule (and Why It's So Critical)

Once you close on the sale of your investment property, the IRS gives you 45 calendar days, *not business days, not "around six weeks," but a firm 45-day window,* to identify the property or properties you intend to purchase as part of your 1031 Exchange. This is one of the most stressful parts of the process for many investors because there are no extensions on this rule. When the clock starts, it cannot be stopped, paused, or renegotiated.

To stay compliant, you must *formally identify* your replacement property in writing (your Qualified Intermediary will give you the official form or format). This identification must be specific—you can't just say "a duplex in Daytona Beach." You must list the property address or parcel number so the IRS knows exactly what you're planning to buy.

To keep the system fair and prevent abuse, the IRS has created a few rules about how many properties you can identify. The three most common identification methods are the Three-Property Rule, the 200% Rule, and (less commonly used) the 95% Rule. For the sake of simplicity and relevance to most investors, here's how the two rules you'll use most often work:

Option 1: The Three-Property Rule (Most Common)

You can identify up to three potential replacement properties, regardless of their price.

- They can be $200,000 each
- They can be $2 million each
- They can be a mix of condos, rentals, land, commercial...

There is *no value limit* under this rule.

This is the simplest and most commonly used option because it gives you flexibility without needing to worry about appraisals or total valuation.

Example: You sell your rental property for $500,000. Within 45 days, you identify:

- a $600,000 beach rental in Flagler Beach
- a $550,000 duplex in Ormond Beach
- a $1.1M quadplex in Palm Coast

These all qualify because there's no limit on combined value when using the Three-Property Rule.

Option 2: The 200% Rule (Used When You Want More Options)

If you want to identify more than three properties, which could be helpful when the market is tight or you're still deciding, you can—but the IRS sets a limit:

The total combined value of *ALL* the properties you identify cannot exceed 200% of the value of the property you sold.

Here's the math:

- You sell a property for $500,000.
- 200% of $500,000 is $1,000,000.
- So you can identify *as many properties as you want*, as long as the combined market value of all properties you list does not exceed $1,000,000.

Example: You sell your rental for $500,000. You want to identify multiple potential properties because inventory is low. You list five properties worth:

$220,000
$180,000
$250,000
$160,000
$170,000

The combined value of the five properties is $980,000. This is less than $1,000,000 ; therefore, this qualifies under the 200% rule.

But if your list totaled $1,020,000, the exchange would be at risk of failing (unless the obscure 95% rule applied which can lead to disqualification or excess scrutiny, so I recommend avoiding that scenario).

Why These Rules Matter So Much

The IRS wants to ensure that investors aren't "window shopping" dozens of properties forever. They need to be sure you are serious about completing the exchange, that there's a clear paper trail of your intentions and that exchanges remain streamlined and compliant

If you fail to identify your replacement properties correctly within the 45 days, *the entire exchange is automatically disqualified.*

Practical Tips for Using the 45-Day Rule Like a Pro

Start looking early. If you know you are getting ready to sell a property, you need to also be getting ready to buy a property in exchange. I have seen several investors sell because they were offered a great price, but then ended up in a jam because they couldn't find a "good" replacement property and ended up buying something they really didn't want. Don't put yourself in that situation. Start looking for the new property the minute you know you are selling the original property.

Over-identify when necessary, using the 3-property rule or the 200% rule. Try to find as many properties as you can that meet your thresholds. You never know if one of them will go under contract while you are still selling or if there will be inspection issues during your inspection period that will make you want to walk away. There are plenty of reasons to have lots of backups...

like the tens to hundreds of thousands of dollars you are spending.

Use a local agent or property manager you trust to help scout properties. Make sure the agent understands the specific rules of a 1031 Exchange. Especially at the beginning of your real estate investing journey, it is crucial to have an agent. Most of the time (though not all so check with your agent), real estate commissions are paid by the seller, not the buyer. So, especially as a buyer, why would anyone not take advantage of the expertise of a real estate agent? A good one will know their market and can help you with running the numbers on your investment property. They will also usually have great connections to contractors, inspectors and other tradespeople you may need along the way.

Stay in constant communication with your Qualified Intermediary and your agent. A missed deadline or misunderstanding can lead to big tax consequences.

How to Find a Qualified 1031 Intermediary

I have found that 1031 Exchange QI's are surprisingly harder to find than expected. You want a bonded, experienced, financial institution-backed intermediary. I would suggest reaching out to local real estate groups or getting on a site like BiggerPockets.com and asking in their forums.

Here are some other places you can search:

- Ask real estate attorneys or your CPA
- Check with reputable title companies or commercial brokers

- Google 1031 specialists
- Federation of Exchange Accommodators (FEA) website
- There are some more well known exchange companies such as IPX 1031, Asset Preservation, Inc., and First American Exchange

Before hiring your QI, be sure to ask:

- How many exchanges have you completed?
- Are you bonded and insured?
- What protections do you have for client funds?
- What is the fee structure?
- How do you handle identification deadlines?
- Do you provide documentation templates?

A reliable QI is worth every penny.

The Cost

Most investors are pleasantly surprised. There are fees associated with these exchanges, but 1031 Exchanges aren't typically expensive. For a standard single-property exchange, expect to pay around $1,000–$1,500; however, times and markets change, so a quick check with ChatGPT should let you know what is typical in your market. Red flag if the QI you choose is charging much more than this.

When To Use a 1031 Exchange

Here are some scenarios that might make a 1031 Exchange a great choice:

You are upgrading your portfolio. I love this option. You buy a small unit, build equity in it, then sell and

1031 the equity. You buy a bigger/better property, using the equity as your down payment but taking on a similar mortgage as you had before ... tada! You now own a bigger, better property and your monthly burden is the same—BUT—your new rent will be likely higher on the new, bigger and better property. Is it just me, or does this remind you of playing Monopoly growing up?

Reduce Headaches. We all end up with a property at some point that is more trouble than it is worth. Save your stress (and your overall health) by dumping bad properties in exchange for properties that don't drive you crazy with issues.

Move Money Into a New Market. Markets are always changing. There will be times that the market you are in no longer makes sense compared to other markets. Don't be afraid to shift equity from a slow-growth area into a hot market. But make sure it makes sense. Sometimes the costs associated outweigh the benefits so check your math before making this move

Consolidate Properties. Now this is true Monopoly-style. You sell multiple properties to buy a larger or more expensive one ... but ... it's harder than it sounds. I would love to do this right now in my portfolio. I have three smaller homes that would be perfect to sell and 1031 into a much larger (you guessed it, vacation) house. But with the time constraints, selling three properties all at once would be so difficult that I may not be able to pull it off. One may sell quickly but, if the others don't, then I am stuck. However, if this opportunity presents itself, it can be a great opportunity for growth. And in my case, a great opportunity to exchange three small houses for a beachfront mansion, which sounds good to me!

Diversify. Tired of residential issues? Change it up, sell your residential and dip your toes into commercial space. Maybe level up from single family homes to a larger apartment complex or an office building.

Example: When a 1031 Makes Sense

Let's say you bought a beach rental ten years ago for $300,000. Today it's worth $550,000. Your gain (minus depreciation recapture) would normally trigger taxes like:

- Long-term capital gains tax
- Depreciation recapture tax
- State taxes (if applicable)

If you sell without a 1031, you might owe $60,000–$90,000+ in taxes.

With a 1031 Exchange?

You roll the entire $550,000 into a $750,000 duplex *and* keep all your equity working for you. Yes, you will have to pay taxes in the long run, not much different than how some traditional retirement plans work, but your money will grow faster, and you will most likely have more of it. I find the more money I have, the less painful paying bills, and taxes, can be. That's how investors think and scale faster.

Scenario	Sell Price	Original Basis	Taxable Gain	Estimated Taxes Owed	Cash Left to Reinvest
Sell **Without** 1031 Exchange	$550,000	$300,000	$250,000	≈ $70,000	≈ $480,000
Sell **With** 1031 Exchange	$550,000	$300,000	deferred	0 (due now)	entire $550,000

A Final Word

A 1031 Exchange isn't just a tax loophole; it's one of the most powerful compounding tools an investor has. When used strategically, it lets you grow bigger, faster, and smarter. And for Boss Lady Investors building long-term wealth? It's a no-brainer strategy to master.

The Bottom Line

♫ *Dance In the Dark* ♫

If there's one thing I want you to take from this chapter, it's this: Don't let money be the reason you don't invest. There are a million paths to property ownership, you just need to find the one that works for you.

These are just *some* of the real estate strategies out there—FHA loans, "subject to" deals, private money, hard money, partnerships, self-directed IRAs—I've used them, learned from them, and built my portfolio around them. But if you fall in love with real estate investing like I have, keep learning as there's a whole world of creative investing techniques out there beyond what I've covered.

The secret? Stay curious. Keep learning. Keep growing.

On a recent retreat, I spent a week snowmobiling with a woman from Texas who specializes in land deals and hard money lending. Now, I don't know a ton about either of those topics, and I definitely don't know the Texas market. But I do know this: she's a Boss Lady extraordinaire. She's making serious money, she's smart, and she's someone I enjoyed being around. That's more than enough for me to pay attention. So, in a few months, I'm hopping on a flight to Texas to spend time with her, walk some land, and learn how she's making her magic happen. Because that's what we do, we stay curious, we stay open, and we stay hungry for new ways to grow.

Here's your Boss Lady reminder: you don't have to know everything to get started. You don't have to have it all figured out. But what you *do* need is the mindset of a learner, the guts to try, and the grit to step into your power. Ask questions. Go to events. Join a mastermind. Take the trip. Read the book (well, you're off to a good start there). Don't wait for perfect because perfect never comes. To paraphrase Theodore Roosevelt: *Start with what you have, where you are, and grow from there.* There are so many ways to build wealth through real estate, and so many ways to fund that growth, you just need the courage to begin and the commitment to keep going.

Get scrappy. Get bold. Get curious. And start asking, "How *can* I make this happen?"

Chapter 9
MONEY CAN'T BUY HAPPINESS

♫ *The Greatest Love of All* ♫

As I sit here writing this final chapter, I'm flying first class. *Again.*

What used to feel like a dream—stretching my legs out, sipping champagne while 30,000 feet in the air, being greeted by name—is now relatively standard. Usually it's first class, but sometimes it's even private. And yes, I still squeal with excitement every time I board a plane where I don't have to go through security. Those coach days though, packed in like a sardine and praying the person in front of me doesn't recline? Thankfully, *only* on the shortest of short flights (hey, I'm still thrifty sometimes even if I don't have to be). Because these days, I've built a life with options.

And Boss Lady, *that's the goal*: a life with options.

This book has shared the tools, strategies, and real-life stories that have helped me create a life filled with choices. Choices about how I spend my time, where I live, what I do with my money, and who I do business with. Real estate has been my major vehicle for scaling up financially, but *mindset* has been my engine. The road hasn't always been smooth—there have been plenty of potholes, detours, times when my business partner took the wheel (and she's a scary driver) and a few fender benders. But I stayed the course. And now, I want the same for you.

Because this journey you're on? It's about so much more than just money. It's about building a life you're proud of. One that feels good when your head hits the pillow at night. One that lets you commit fully to yourself, your family, and your purpose.

Real Talk: Money & Happiness

When people say to me, "Money can't buy happiness," I will argue that's not 100% true. What I think they might really mean is that money doesn't *guarantee* you happiness. That is 100% true.

Here are some things money *can* buy: Options. Peace of mind. Comfort. Freedom. The ability to say yes to the vacation, the retreat, the new home, the time off when you need it most. Money, when managed wisely, creates the space for happiness to flourish. It lets you spend your time how you want, be present with the people you love, and support the causes you care about. It's not the only way to be happy, but it's one hell of a powerful tool to help you build a joyful, intentional life.

Let me tell you what financial freedom really feels like. It's not just about being able to afford luxury. It's about waking up in the morning and knowing your bills are covered. It's about saying "yes" to the things that light you up, like booking that last-minute girls' trip or flying your parents in for the holidays. It's about saying "no" to what no longer serves you, whether that's a toxic client, a draining job, or a life that feels too small.

Financial freedom means presence. It means you're not sitting on the sidelines of your kids' lives. You're not watching your grandkids grow up through FaceTime. You're living. Fully. And with intention.

But here's the truth that matters even more: your *mindset* is what creates happiness. If you wake up every day blaming others, waiting for permission, or expecting success to knock on your door without effort, you're already behind. The mindset of a winner starts with accountability. With hustle. With grit. It's waking up early to chase your goals and staying up late when you need to. It's putting in the extra reps at the gym, the extra calls to lock in that deal, the extra hours learning something new.

Look at Olympic athletes. Lindsay Vonn didn't win medals by sleeping in and scrolling Instagram. She trained. She fell. She got back up. She visualized success and did the work, again and again. That's what champions do. You can be the champion of your life.

This journey requires more than investing in property; it requires investing in yourself. I'm gonna get on a little soap box here because I truly care about you and want you to have the *best life ever.* The journey requires that you take care of *yourself.* That means being in healthy relationships. That means taking care of your mind, your soul, *your body*. It's pretty hard to work on a renovation or to decorate a vacation rental if you get winded just walking up stairs. So yes, take the yoga class. Go to the gym. For me, Pilates has been life changing for my mental health and flexibility. I hit the gym at least four days a week for cardio and weights. I eat food to fuel my body. I rest when I need to. I don't make excuses, and I promise, I have less free time than most. Your body is your machine—keep it sharp and strong.

We all only have twenty-four hours in a day. Even our rockstar women referenced throughout the book. If *they* can make time for health, *so can you.*

You've likely already heard that you are the sum of the five people you spend the most time with, so *choose wisely.* Surround yourself with Boss Ladies who lift you up and push you forward. If your friends, partner, or spouse are holding you back—rethink those relationships or find ways to work on them. If you have a circle that promotes your dreams, supports your hustle, and reminds you of your power? *Lean in.* That kind of support is gold.

Please, don't be the woman who lives online blaming external forces for everything wrong in her life. I've seen women on social media blaming political parties for their finances, for housing prices, even for natural disasters. I've watched people attack their spouses or friends in public posts. Don't be her. Be the woman known for finding a way through the chaos. The phoenix rising from the ashes. The lioness who survives the drought, defends her territory, and roars with purpose.

And once you start to reach this level, another truth will become very clear: those of us that make it here have a responsibility to lead. To stand tall for other women. To pave the path for those just getting started. *Because if we don't, who will?*

That's why my business partner Kym and I created Girls Gone Adventuring Retreats. We wanted to bring women together from all walks of life to not only explore the world, but to explore what's possible for themselves.

We learn from each other. On those trips, I think we get more out of it than our attendees do. We get to sit in rooms, in beautiful settings, with other women as they strategize, learn and make connections with women, *just like them*. Smart. Strategic. Powerful. We connect over our shared drive and our desire to lift other women up. We stay in each other's lives, even if for some it's just on social media, so that we can cheer each other on. Some of us become lifelong friends, business partners, golf buddies. Boss Ladies, stay curious. We keep learning. We grow, together.

A few weeks after returning from our snowmobiling GGAR trip, I posted on social media about an underfunded school I'd been supporting. The kids there needed shoes, just basic shoes that fit. I asked my community if anyone could spare $10 or $25 to help. The Texan, the Boss Lady I told you about, saw my post. She then Venmo'd me enough money to buy **every single child** at the school a pair of shoes. She lives in another state, she will never meet these children, nor will she win a plaque to put on her wall because she donated. She did it because *she could*. Because that's what Boss Ladies do. We rise, but we also reach back. We give. We impact. *We matter.*

Charitable giving isn't optional for me anymore. It's a core part of my mission. Whether it's donating time, money, or mentorship, giving back is how we multiply our blessings. And when you build a life rooted in abundance, it becomes second nature to share it.

Now let's talk about legacy. What we're doing here isn't just for fun. It's for our families. It's for our communities. It's for our future. We are building **generational wealth** that will change the trajectory of our lives and the lives of those who come after us. Imagine your grandkids living debt-free, empowered to chase their passions because of the decisions you made today. That's what we're working toward.

You are not meant to live a life of limitation. You are not meant to simply survive. You are meant to thrive. To build. To create. To lead.

So set the goals. Dream big. Dream **bigger** than you think is reasonable. And then? Take one step at a time.

Keep learning. Keep leveling up. Keep investing—in real estate, in your community, in yourself.

Keep your word.

The world needs more women who know their worth, build wealth, and give generously. The future generations need to have even more opportunities than we did. Our sisters before us fought like the divas they were to get us a seat at the table.

We belong there. We deserve to be there. And we must make sure that the women after us have even more seats.

You are minutes away from finishing a book about real estate investing. Do you know the class that puts you in? You are part of a group of women that are empowering their financial, emotional and social lives. You are building generational wealth—for your family, for causes you care about and maybe even for the children of your children's children that will only know you from the legacy.

In the end, isn't that what it's all about? Leaving a legacy. Leaving something for the next generations to look up to. Leaving the world better than you found it.

We talked a lot about women being great investors, but more importantly, we have great hearts and so much love to give. That's the final superpower of this book (but we have so many more). It's our hearts. There is a reason we didn't talk about becoming slumlords or ways to cheap out on our tenants. We talked about ways to make things nicer than we found them. We figured out ways to create spaces for families to call *home*.

It's time. It's time to take your superpowers and spread your wings, Boss Lady. Create the strategy, build the empire, leave the legacy.

There is a little girl out there that needs you to lead the way, to believe in yourself, for her. For *our* future.

Boss Lady, you did it. You finished a book about real estate investing, something only a tiny fraction of the *world* will ever do. You have the tools, you have the mindset and most importantly, you have the heart.

You, my friend, are a Boss Lady Real Estate Investor.

Now go live like one. Go show the world.

All my love.

You got this.

Krista

Afterword

♫ I Get a Kick Out of You ♫

Boss Ladies don't wait for perfect conditions, they create them. In fact, one of my real estate investing partners and I took the opportunities we found in vacation rentals and took it one step further.

That retreat I mentioned where I met the Texan? It was a retreat hosted by our company *Girls Gone Adventuring Retreats*, and if you're wondering what that's all about, let me fill you in. This is our passion project turned powerhouse community. *Girls Gone Adventuring Retreats* is a company my bestie (the one that I also invest in properties with) and I founded to bring together bold, adventurous women who are ready to step out of their comfort zones, try new things, and connect with like-minded souls while exploring the world. We do all of this while talking money, sharing investing strategies and educating one another.

We've hiked glaciers in Montana, fished for salmon in Alaska, rode ATVs through Costa Rica, soaked up the energy of New Mexico, climbed red rocks in Sedona, scalloped in Florida, safaried through Kenya and surfed waves in Portugal. These retreats are equal parts fun, growth, connection, and empowerment. We mix in personal development, goal setting, and the kind of wild, wonderful experiences that shake up your soul in the best way.

And yes, you're invited. Whether you want to climb a mountain, conquer a fear, or just hang with other badass women and laugh until your stomach hurts, there's a spot for you. You can find upcoming trips and all the details at www.girlsgoneadventuring.com, or follow us on Instagram @girlsgoneadventuring. Come join us—you never know what new ideas, business partners, or next big moves might come from one incredible week with the right tribe.

The added benefit, outside of hanging with my new besties, traveling the world and experiencing incredible adventures? We get to check out real estate in amazing locales and find places outside the US to invest. Once you step into that world, you may find even more financing options (and opportunities).

Tools And Resources

Your go-to toolbox for
building wealth, scaling smart,

REAL ESTATE SEARCH & DEAL ANALYSIS

Zillow / Redfin / Realtor.com, Great for initial property scouting, comparable sales (comps), and neighborhood research.

BiggerPockets. Free calculators, investor forums, networking groups, and educational content.

PropStream. Pull leads, comps, off-market data, tax records, lien info, and motivated seller lists.

Mashvisor. Powerful rental analysis tool for both long-term and short-term rental projections.

AirDNA. The best data platform for evaluating short-term rental income, occupancy, and demand.

Rentometer. Quickly determine competitive long-term rental rates in your target market.

FINANCING AND LOAN SHOPPING

Bankrate Mortgage Calculator. Run quick monthly payments and affordability checks.

NerdWallet Mortgage Comparisons. Compare conventional, HELOC, and refinancing options across lenders.

LenderFi / Rocket Mortgage / Movement Mortgage. Fast online pre-approvals for conventional, FHA, and refi scenarios.

Visio Lending & Kiavi. Popular for DSCR loans and investor-friendly underwriting.

Local Credit Unions. Often provide lower HELOC rates, portfolio loans, and flexible underwriting.

BUDGETING, ACCOUNTING AND CASH FLOW

QuickBooks Online. Best for managing income, expenses, receipts, and year-end tax reports.

Stessa (Recommended!). FREE property management accounting platform built for real estate investors.

BiggerPockets Calculators. Analyze flips, BRRRRs, rentals, and 1031 strategies with ease.

Google Sheets / Excel Templates. Simple and customizable worksheets for tracking numbers.

RENOVATION, CONTRACTORS & PROPERTY CARE

Thumbtack. Find reliable contractors, handymen, cleaners, and specialty trades.

Angi (formerly Angie's List). Detailed reviews and verified local service providers.

Home Depot Pro & Lowe's Pro. Access bulk pricing, rebates, and contractor-grade materials.

HomeBinder. Keep digital "house manuals," maintenance logs, appliance warranties, and receipts.

DUE DILIGENCE & TRANSACTION

JotForm or Google Forms. Helpful for collecting tenant information and screening details.

DocuSign. Secure electronic signing for leases, offers, and partnership agreements.

PandaDoc. Templates for contracts, operating agreements, and legal forms.

Title Company / Attorney. Your best friend during closings, title searches, and 1031 compliance.

PROPERTY MANAGEMENT

Avail. Great for self-managing long-term rentals — screening, rent collection, leases.

Buildium / AppFolio. Full-service platforms for larger portfolios (10+ doors).

Hostaway. Short-term rental automation (guest messaging, pricing, cleaners, calendars).

PriceLabs / Wheelhouse. Dynamic pricing tools to maximize STR revenue.

Ring Cameras + Keyless Smart Locks (Schlage, Yale, August). Essential for security and remote guest/tenant access.

VACATION RENTAL ESSENTIALS

(Boss Lady Style!)

AirDNA. Industry standard for STR market projections.

Canva Pro. Design listing photos, house manuals, checklists, Instagram content, and digital guides.

Amazon Storefront Essentials. Stock your STR with high-quality linens, durable kitchenware, and guest amenities.

NoiseAware. Protect your rental with noise monitoring that avoids parties.

Minut Sensor. Great for temperature, humidity, motion, and noise monitoring.

LEGAL, INSURANCE & PROTECTION

LLC Formation: LegalZoom or Your Local Attorney. Set up proper business structure for liability protection.

Rocket Lawyer / Nolo. Templates for partnership agreements, lease addendums, and notices.

Umbrella Insurance (Highly Recommended!). Inexpensive extra liability coverage protecting your personal assets.

Landlord Insurance Providers. State Farm, USAA, Travelers, Allstate, Foremost.

EDUCATION & TRAINING

Books

Rich Dad Poor Dad, by Robert Kiyosaki

The Book on Rental Property Investing, by Brandon Turner

The Millionaire Real Estate Investor, by Gary Keller

Build a Rental Property Empire, by Mark Ferguson

Your Books! (*Becoming a Boss Lady Investor* & *The Boss Lady Real Estate Investor*)

Podcasts

BiggerPockets

Real Estate Rookie

Wealth Without Wall Street

The Short-Term Show

Girls Gone Adventuring (👀 future plug?)

Masterminds & Local Groups

REIA (Real Estate Investor Association)

Women in Real Estate (WIRE) Networks

Local meetups & chambers of commerce

PROFESSIONAL SERVICES

(Build Your Dream Team)

CPA (Real Estate-Savvy). Crucial for tax strategy, depreciation, 1031 guidance, and entity planning.

Real Estate Attorney. Contracts, partnerships, seller financing, subject-to deals.

Insurance Broker. Helps compare landlord and STR policies.

Real Estate Agent / Broker (Investor-Friendly). Someone who understands cash flow, comps, and renovations — not just pretty kitchens.

Property Manager (If you don't self-manage). Great for scaling and avoiding burnout.

BOSS LADY MUST-HAVES

Vision Board (Physical or Digital via Canva). Keep your goals in front of you.

Accountability Partner or Investment Buddy. Someone who pushes you, supports you, and grows with you.

Girls Gone Adventuring Retreats. Because investing + travel + badass women = magic

A Notebook or Digital App for Ideas. You'll get million-dollar ideas in random places. Capture everything.

FINANCING OPTIONS FOR REAL ESTATE INVESTORS

Loan Type	Down Payment	Credit Requirements	Income Verification	Typical Interest Rates	Best For
Conventional Loan	15–25% (investment)	620+ 700+ (better terms)	Yes (W-2s, tax returns)	Lowest (if you qualify)	Primary home, 2nd home, 1–4 unit rentals
FHA / VA Loan	FHA: 3.5% VA: 0%	FHA: 580+ VA: flexible	Yes (must occupy as primary)	Low, government-backed	House hacking
Creative Financing (Seller financing, Subject To, Lease-to-Own)	Negotiable (5–20% typical)	Flexible (depends on seller)	Usually No	Flexible / negotiated	Investors without traditional approval
DSCR Loan	20–25%	620+ 700+ (better terms)	No (property qualifies itself)	1–3% higher than conventional	Short-term rentals, scaling portfolio
HELOC	N/A	Varies by bank	Tied to property value	4.99 - 12%	Quick purchase, or one that requires cash
Private Money	Negotiatedm (often 10–25%)	Based on relationship/trust	Usually No	6–12% (varies widely)	Flips, small projects, bridge loans
Hard Money	20–30%	Credit less important (asset-based)	Usually No	8–15% (very high)	Flips, distressed properties, BRRRR
Partnerships	Negotiated	N/A (partner fills gaps)	Depends on structure	N/A (depends on financing used)	Scaling without all cash/credit yourself
Self-Directed IRA	N/A	N/A	N/A	N/A	Alll types of investment rentals
1031 Exchange	N/A	N/A	N/A	N/A	Alll types of investment rentals

Acknowledgments

To my husband, thank you for giving me the space to write, to dream, and to be unapologetically me. Your steady support, your patience, and your belief in every wild idea I chase make everything in these pages possible. You've held down the fort more times than I can count, and you've never once asked me to shrink so the world could feel more comfortable. Thank you for loving me big enough to let me soar.

To Kym, the best business partner any woman could ever ask for, thank you for understanding that the mission isn't always black and white. You've stood beside me through every pivot, every lesson, every crazy new project, always believing that together we can help more women build wealth, confidence, and freedom. Thank you for being completely aligned in the belief that leading with kindness and lifting others up is how we make the world better. Your loyalty, your brilliance, and your heart are woven into everything we create.

And to Mary—my editor, my sanity keeper, my gentle nudge forward when my schedule gets chaotic—thank you for pushing me to keep going. Thank you for navigating my timetable with grace, for catching every detail I miss, and for always finding a way to make my words stronger. You are truly the best editor ever, and this book is better because of you.

To each of you, thank you for believing in this vision, in this work, and in me. This book is a testament to the power of a team that dreams boldly, works relentlessly, and lifts women higher every chance we get.

About the Author

Krista Goodrich is a real estate investor, entrepreneur, speaker, and the powerhouse behind *The Boss Lady Investor* brand. From overcoming personal challenges to building a thriving real estate and investment portfolio, Krista has dedicated her life to teaching women how to build wealth, create financial independence, and design a life they love.

She is the founder of numerous businesses in property management, travel & tourism and several other lifestyle and investment ventures rooted in empowerment, community, and adventure.

A lifelong learner and mentor, Krista serves her community through leadership, volunteer initiatives, and advocacy.

When she's not writing, investing, or helping others build their own paths to financial freedom, you'll find Krista traveling the world, hosting women's adventure retreats, renovating another beach house, or enjoying time with her daughter Tiana and her growing family.

Krista believes that wealth is not just money—it's freedom, courage, and the power to lift up the next generation. Through her books, coaching, and platforms, she continues her mission: **to help every woman become the boss of her money, her future, and her life.**

instagram.com/thebossladyinvestor
facebook.com/krista.d.goodrich
tiktok.com/middleagedadventurechick
youtube.com/@thebossladyinvestor

Also by KRISTA GOODRICH

Books *(Available on Amazon)*

Becoming a Boss Lady Investor

Becoming a Boss Lady Real Estate Investor

Becoming a Boss Lady Real Estate Investor Workbook

Websites

www.GirlsGoneAdventuringRetreats.com

www.TheBossLadyInvestor.com

www.MySaltyDogVacation.com

Podcasts

The Boss Lady Investor Podcast

https://www.thebossladyinvestor.com/podcast

YouTube

The Boss Lady Investor channel

https://www.youtube.com/@thebossladyinvestor

Made in United States
Orlando, FL
07 January 2026

76411868R00154